Abby Morton Diaz

The Cats' Arabian Nights

King Grimalkum

Abby Morton Diaz

The Cats' Arabian Nights
King Grimalkum

ISBN/EAN: 9783744762335

Printed in Europe, USA, Canada, Australia, Japan

Cover: Foto ©Thomas Meinert / pixelio.de

More available books at **www.hansebooks.com**

WHEN SHE WAS SEWING I JUMPED UPON HER SHOULDER. (*Page* 14.)

THE
CATS' ARABIAN NIGHTS

OR

KING GRIMALKUM

BY ABBY MORTON DIAZ

PROFUSELY ILLUSTRATED
BY FRANCIS, BOZ, PALMER COX, AND OTHERS

BOSTON
D. LOTHROP COMPANY

CONTENTS.

HOW IT HAPPENED.

One evening when a company of children and older people were looking at funny cat-pictures and telling cat-stories, a little ten-year-old girl asked: " Why can there not be a Cats' Arabian Nights Story Book?"

" There would have to be a Cat King, or Emperor, or Sultan," said her next older sister.

" And a Cat Queen, or Empress, or Sultaness," said their cousin Joe, the sailor.

" And she would have to go on, and on, and on, and on, and on, and on, and on, telling stories in order to save her own life," said their cousin Lucia.

" I propose," said uncle Fred, " that cousin Lucia put together a Cats' Arabian Nights for little children, and have it ready to read to our little children when they all shall come next summer with their fathers and mothers."

" Oh yes! Yes! Do! Pray do! Won't you do it? Say you will! Say you will!" cried many voices.

" I think it will be fun to do it," said cousin Lucia, " if you allow me to put in some make believe and nonsense, if I want to."

" Certainly!" was the cry. " Put in anything. Anything you please!"

Cousin Lucia said she was willing to try, and thus it happened that the summer-children and others got a story book beginning, as all story books should begin, with — once upon a time.

KING GRIMALKUM AND PUSSYANITA;

OR,

THE CATS' ARABIAN NIGHTS.

NCE upon a time the aged Tommo-
bus, King of the Cats, went forth a
hunting and returned with a wound
which caused his death. So Tommo-
bus died and Grimalkum the Powerful
became King in his stead.

King Grimalkum was of course jet black all over
without a single white hair, or he could not have been
made king, and his eyes were of the true royal yellow.

The first act of King Grimalkum's reign was one of
cruelty. He sent forth an order declaring that black,
maltese, and gray, were the only colors to be allowed for
cats, and that all cats which were white or yellow, or
which had more white or yellow hairs than dark ones

should not be permitted to live.   Judges were appointed to measure the spots.

This order caused great affright among the lighter cats.   The wholly white and wholly yellow hid themselves or fled to distant places, and the partly white and partly yellow went in haste to have their dark spots measured by the judges.

Among those who came before the judges was Pussyanita, a beautiful creature just out of kittenhood.   Her playfulness and sweet disposition made her beloved by all.

Alas! it was soon made known by the judges that the dark of Pussyanita measured many less hairs than her white ones.   This caused great sorrow, and King Grimalkum was begged to spare her life.

"Spare her life!   Not if she were twenty Pussyanitas!" cried the King; which was a foolish answer, since she could not have been twenty Pussyanitas, or even nineteen.

Now this sweet and gentle creature was so much beloved, that no one could be found willing to hurt a single hair of her.   When King Grimalkum heard this he became furious with anger, and commanded that she be brought to him at once, saying that he himself would attend to the business, and make quick work of it.   So the lovely Pussyanita was brought before the King.

Her loveliness did not soften his heart; on the contrary he was made more furious than ever by seeing that she sat licking her fur as quietly as if sitting in her own sunny garden spot.

"What are you doing that for, you silly thing?" he cried. "Don't you know you have but a few moments to live?"

"Yes, your majesty," replied the lovely Pussyanita, "but I cannot endure a speck of dirt, and with good reason, for in me you see a descendant, and great, great, great, great, great, twenty-seven times great grandchild of the unhappy and happy Pinky-white. Your majesty must have heard of Pinky-white."

"Never," said the king, sternly. "But why do you call her unhappy and happy? There is no sense in that."

"She was not unhappy and happy at the same time," said Pussyanita. "She was first unhappy and afterwards happy."

"How was that?" asked the king. "And supposing you *are* the great, great, great, great, great, twenty-seven times great granddaughter of Pinky-white, what has that to do with your being unable to endure a speck of dirt?"

Said the lovely Pussyanita, "It would give me pleasure, your majesty, to explain why my great, great, great, great, great, twenty-seven times great grandmother was first unhappy, and why she was afterwards happy, also suppos-ing I *am* the great, great, great, great, great, twenty-seven times great granddaughter of Pinky-white, what that has to do with my being unable to endure a speck of dirt; it would give me pleasure, I say, to explain all this, but it would take a longer time than I have to live."

"Time shall be granted you," said the king, "for I am curious to know why your great, great, great, great, great, twenty-seven times great grandmother Pinky-white was unhappy and why she was happy, and to know why your being her great, great, great, great, great, twenty-seven times great granddaughter should be a reason why you are unable to endure a speck of dirt."

"At your majesty's request," replied Pussyanita, "I will tell you the story of my great, great, great, great, great, twenty-seven times great grandmother Pinky-white, as she herself told it, when ordered to do so, at Lady Yellowpaw's famous party."

"Stop!" cried the king. "Why was your great, great, great, great, great, twenty-seven times great grandmother Pinky-white ordered to tell her story at Lady Yellow-paw's famous party? Who was Lady Yellow-paw? Why was her party famous?"

"Please your majesty," replied Pussyanita, "I shall be happy to explain to your majesty who was Lady Yellow-paw, and why her party was famous, and why my great, great, great, great, great, twenty-seven times great grandmother Pinky-white was ordered to tell her story at that party, but your majesty must perceive that to do all this will require much time."

"Begin then!" cried the king. "Begin with your Lady Yellow-paw and her famous party, and then go on to your twenty-seven times great grandmother; and do not waste time waiting or waste words in the telling."

The lovely Pussyanita bowed and began with Lady Yellow-paw and her famous party, and then went on to tell the story of Pinky-white as told by herself at that famous party.

THE STORY OF PINKY-WHITE.

"The first that I knew of myself, I found myself by
the side of my mother, among some hay in a basket
along with three other kittens of my own age and size.
Two of our number were quickly stolen from us. It will
thus be seen that I had scarcely begun to live before I
began to be unhappy. As I grew older I became more
and more unhappy, for the place was cold, the floor was
hard, our mother cuffed us, and girl-Mary, who owned
us, knew not the best way of stroking.

"One day when girl-Mary sat by our basket, girl-Jane
came down there bringing her own cat and kittens. Girl-
Jane had called to see us many times, and I had been
pleased with the looks of her face, and the sounds of her
voice, and the touches of her fingers; and she knew the
best way of stroking.

"Girl-Jane was smaller than girl-Mary, but she knew

GIRL-JANE AND GIRL-MARY.

more. Girl-Jane said she wanted girl-Mary to change kittens with her. She wanted me and Minnie because we were whiter than her kittens.

"'No, Jane,' said girl-Mary, 'I can't change, for you know mine are all named, and besides your cat would not like it. She knows what we are talking about. Don't you see how anxious she looks?'

"It made me unhappy to hear this. I wanted to go with girl-Jane, away from the cold place, and the hard floor, and my cross mother and be stroked the best way. Minnie too wished to go. She cried when girl-Mary gave back the other kittens. As for me, I could only turn away and hide my sorrowful face.

" My next unhappiness was the unhappiness of being whipped with a rod. An old lady wished for a cat to catch her mice and thought she would take a kitten and teach it to behave well. I was carried to her home. I had here a warm place, and a carpet, and the old lady did not stroke at all, so that I was not made unhappy by bad stroking. But my unhappiness was great, on account of the rod. It was rod here and rod there; rod on the pantry shelf and rod on the chair-cushion; rod on the parlor sofa and rod on the best bed; rod at the milk pitcher, and rod at the custard-pie.

"A greater unhappiness must now be told. For this

greater unhappiness was the cause of another unhappiness even greater than this — oh, very much greater! It was the cause of a long and dreadful unhappiness in which I nearly starved to death. It was something which would make any and every cat unhappy. It was this. I could not catch well. Mice, birds, moles, bats, squirrels, rabbits, almost always got away from me. I think I must have been born short-clawed.

WELL MADE FOR CATCHING.

"In a corner of the garden was a chicken-coop. This chicken-coop was well made for catching. It would seem that all a cat need do was to lie quietly on top, looking over the edge, and when a chicken popped out, spring and catch it. Any other cat would have done all this. The next house cat did do all this. I did not do all this. I lay quietly on top of the chicken-coop. I looked over the edge, and when a chicken popped out I sprang. I did everything the next house cat did *except* to catch the chicken.

" I had the same luck in fishing. There was a stream at the bottom of our garden and at its edge were large mossy rocks on which a cat might stretch herself in the sun, or if the day were hot she might lie in their cool shade. Trees grew near by and any other cat would have often caught a bird among their branches. The next house cat did this. I did not do this. Any other cat than myself would have now and then

I DID MY BEST.

caught a fish in the stream at the foot of the rocks. The next house cat did this. I did not do this. I often lay close to the water — as shown how to do by the next house cat, and watched the fishes as they glided past. When one rose to the top I did my best to catch it, but even did I have the luck to touch one, it was sure to slip out and away. I used to think sometimes that if fishes had not been made so slippery I could have held on, but then the next house cat held on to slippery fishes. I am almost sure I must have been born short-clawed.

"As for squirrels and rabbits, they seemed at last to be not a bit afraid of me, even when I had become a full-grown cat. One saucy squirrel used to tease me by coming very near and then darting out of my reach. This squirrel became very bold. He even popped in at the doors and windows. One day when I was asleep on the sofa by the library window, he ran as near me as the back of the sofa — bold little thing! and by the time I had turned over he was out of the window, and I soon got sight of his bushy tail whisking through the tall tree-

BOLD LITTLE THING!

tops, and of his little bright eyes looking down at me through the leaves. He would not have got away so easily from the next house cat. There can be no doubt but that I must have been born short-clawed.

"The next house cat caught mice. I did not. I might have caught some had not the mouse-holes been made so small. But then the next house cat had the same kind of mouse-holes I had.

"Sometimes I thought if I had been a Tabby I might

THE NEXT HOUSE CAT

have caught as well as the next house cat. But then I could not be a Tabby.

"One day — oh unhappy day! the next house cat's mistress came to see my mistress, and they talked of cats.

I lay outside under the open window and heard every word, and understood. Mistresses, as you very well know, dear Lady Yellow-paw — as all of you at this famous party very well know — mistresses have no idea how much their cats can understand.

"Said my mistress, ' Pinky-white is the neatest cat that ever was seen. She will have no dirt on her fur. She licks off every speck. She keeps herself snow white. And I have taught her to behave well. I no longer keep a rod. But she catches no mice.'

"'You feed her too well,' said the next house-cat's mistress. 'Send her to Miss Rhody and get you a mouser. Miss Rhody is out of a cat and is waiting to find a neat one. Miss Rhody has managed cats these forty years and knows how to do it. Miss Rhody never feeds a cat. If it won't catch mice she drowns it.'

"' I will send Pinky-white to Miss Rhody to-morrow,' said my mistress.

"This frightened me. Oh what should I do? What could I do? In my agony of distress I ran round and round in a circle in the potato patch, tore up the squash vines, and at last I sprang over the high wall, and in that house and garden I was never seen more.

"Then began the terrible unhappiness of my life. No tongue can tell what I suffered. Hiding behind fences,

BUT ALAS! THREE OTHERS WERE GNAWING THE BONE.

under barns, in empty pig-styes, empty hen-houses; being driven from back doors, hooted at by boys, barked at by dogs, and hungry, hungry, hungry, oh so hungry!—for I could not catch well—and always dirty! Ah! none who have not felt it can know the unhappiness of a cat without a home!

"One night I thought surely I should taste a bit of meat. A black and white kitten kindly told me of a large bone she had seen in a yard, and we scampered to that yard. But alas! three others were already gnawing the bone and there was nothing on the bone, for a tommy cat had kept the others away till he had eaten off all the meat and then he sat seeing them gnaw the bare bone. I did not gnaw. I did not wish to gnaw bare bone.

"One day a dreadful thing happened to me. It was when I was hungrier than I had ever been before, though I had been very hungry. I was so hungry I thought I could not live, and I went into the fields to try to catch something. It was a silly thing for me to try to catch a rat when I was short-clawed.

"I did. A great rat went into a field and I thought, oh if I could only get that rat! I *must* have that rat! I *must!*

"I put myself down flat and crept behind that rat. He went creeping through some wheat and corn and I crept behind, quicker than he, for I could creep quicker.

He went up a large stalk to his nest. I sprang up and grabbed him, but alas! I could not take good hold and he got away and sprang at me and the mother rat sprang out at me and they bit me, and would have killed me, but I got away and ran with all my might, and lay down under some bushes, and pretty soon that same black and white kitten came and licked the blood off me and brought me a mole to eat, or I never should have stirred from that spot.

"As the weather grew colder I suffered more and more. I longed for a home.

"Often at evening I ran behind persons hoping to be invited to their houses, but they always drove me back.

"During all this time I was obliged to endure the distress of knowing that my fur was not perfectly clean.

"When winter came my unhappiness was greater than it had ever been before, though it had already been very great.

"But one day, oh joyful day! my unhappiness came to an end, oh joyful end! I will tell how this happened.

"The ground was covered with snow, slosh and mud. I had been running hither and thither, under barns, in coal cellars, and in other places trying to catch something, but having had the misfortune, as I have already told your ladyship, the misfortune of being born short-

HE WENT UP A LARGE STALK TO HIS NEST.

clawed, I had caught nothing. Begrimed with dirt,

hungry, cold, for-
lorn, I was on my
way to my jump-
ing spot. This was
the corner of a wall
near a back door.
It was also near to
some bushes and
trees all snugly
fenced in, and un-
der these I had of-
ten hid myself and
tried to clean my
fur and watched
for the back door
to open. I called it
my jumping spot
because s o m e-
times I jumped
from that spot and
got in at the back
door and snatched
a bit from the

THE KIND MAIDEN.

plate of the cat which belonged to the house. Sometimes a

kind maiden had thrown me scraps from one of the windows.

"Now just as I was to jump from my jumping spot I saw this kind maiden coming down the steps. She had her pet kitten in her arms and was tending it with care. 'Oh pet kitten! pet kitten!' I mewed to it. 'How little you know the unhappiness of a cat without a home!' Mewing this, I hung my tail and was slinking out of sight when I heard these words.

"'Puss! Puss! Pussy! Pussy! Puss!' How I wished I could think they were spoken to me! 'Pussy! Poor Pussy! Here Pussy!' I turned my head, but kept moving. 'Pussy! Pussy! Pussy! Puss! Poor Pussy! Pussy! Pussy! Here Pussy! Poor Pussy!' I stopped.

"'Pussy! Here Pussy! come Pussy!'

"Yes! they were—they were spoken to me! She was looking at me! 'Good old Pussy! come here, good old Pussy!'

"She held out her hand. I dared not go. She went in and placed a saucer of milk on the kitchen hearth, called me and left the door open, and went to another room. I crept in to the hearth, and lapped, lapped, lapped, oh how I did lap! No tongue can tell the sweetness of that milk!

"As soon as I had eaten the milk I examined the things in the room, then I rolled over and over on the door mat to get the coal dust off, then I sat on the hearth

SHE TOOK ME UP

and licked myself clean. The cook came in and shook the broom at me and cried: 'Scat! Scat!' Just then the kind maiden showed her face at the door. 'Here's a strange cat!' the cook said to her. 'We don't want another cat!'

"'Why! how white and clean she has made herself,' said the maiden. 'She is a neat cat. I have often seen her cleaning herself out under the bushes. I mean to keep her. She is just the cat for poor Ellen.'

"I went and rubbed against her clothes, rubbed hard, and tried to purr loud enough to make her understand that I said in purr language, 'I love you, love you. Don't send me away!'

"Oh the happiness of a cat with a good home! I had now a good home. I was held in laps, stroked well, talked to, even kissed. I had warm milk, meat scraps, and plenty of fish. I was not expected to catch. I wonder why cats are almost always expected to catch.

"I went every day to see poor Ellen. I used to go up after breakfast and scratch the door and get myself let in. When she combed her hair I sat close to her looking-glass, and looked at her while she combed her hair, and when she sat down to rest I lay on the floor and waited, and when she put on her shoes I kept at her feet, and rubbed her feet, and then I rubbed against her a good

deal and purred to be taken up, and she took me up.
Poor Ellen could not walk much but she could hold me.
She liked me because I kept myself so clean and white.

"The maiden said she never before saw a cat which
could not endure a speck of dirt. She said she believed

THE HEN'S LESSON IN NEATNESS.

I taught her other cats to be neat. This might not
have been true, but it was certainly true that while I was
with them the other cats were very careful to clean
themselves after eating. One day she called the family
to see us. 'Look!' she cried. 'Look at my cat that

cannot endure a speck of dirt! I do believe that rooster has brought his hen to make her take a lesson in neatness.'

"This might not have been true, either. He might have brought her to make her take a lesson in neatness, or he might have brought her for the scraps we often left.

"Speaking of hens, a chicken made something happen to me which does not often happen to a cat. Our hen hatched out a brood of chickens and while they were little she was carried off by a fox. All the chickens died except two, and one of these had a weak throat. When the fox carried off the hen he stepped on that little chicken's neck and it had a weak throat ever after. One day when I was in a far corner of the garden I heard a curious noise like a choking, or a peeping, but more like a choking than a peeping. I watched, and presently that little chicken came out of the grass. I should have sprung upon it if I had not seen that it was in distress and was coming to me for help. It had got a bug stuck in its throat. It came close to me and I licked it, and purred to it and tried to cover it over with myself just as its own mother used to. Pretty soon it swallowed that bug.

"After this it often came to me to be licked and purred to when it had a bug or a worm stuck in its

throat, and at last it brought the other chicken, and I
tried to be a mother to them both, for my dear little
kittens had all been sent away.   The other chicken
grew faster than the
first one ; it had a strong
throat to swallow with.
I took great care of
them both and licked
them clean, for I could
not bear a speck of dirt

I TRIED TO BE A MOTHER TO THEM BOTH.

on them any more than if they had been my kittens.

"Now when the maiden saw me doing this she told
her brother that if I could live peaceably with chickens I
could with birds, and that she meant to try me.   She
first fed me well then brought to me a tame bird.   Its
wings had been clipped so that it could not fly and it was
very hungry.   It was afraid of me and it hopped round
crying its bird kind of cry.   But I did not touch it and
when it saw me licking the chicken it hopped near me to
get some rice which both the chickens were eating.   In
a few days the bird and I were good friends.   He let me
lick him and he used to sit on my head and sing, and we
all ate our meals together until the chickens died.   The
first one died of its weak throat and the other died of the
bite of a cat.   One day a girl brought her cat to see us.

THE HAPPY FAMILY.

She kept her up high on her shoulders, away from us, but when that other chicken put its head out to pick up a bug, that cat jumped down quick and caught that chicken by the head, and it died afterwards.

"But before these died the maiden and her brother tamed some young guinea pigs and some young white mice, and made them grow up friends. They stayed in a pen close to ours until we all became acquainted with each other and then the slats between the pens were taken off, and the two pens were made into one and we all lived together. I must own that at first I did wish to catch a mouse just for the sake of catching one, and though born short-clawed I could no doubt have caught one in a pen, but the maiden thought I might have such a wish and pared my claws. I was very happy with my new friends. After I knew the little mice I had no wish to catch them. I played with them and let them run over my back. When one comes to know mice, one likes their company and finds them very agreeable and playful and lively.

"The maiden's brother said they might as well have a Happy Family, and he trained some big birds and other birds and they came to live with us and we were a very Happy Family.

"When the maiden and her brother went away to live

in another place they sold us to a showman to put in his show. The showman travels about the country showing his show. A few days ago the wagon we were in upset and our door came open. The birds flew away, the mice hid under a rock and the guinea pigs ran into the woods. I am on my way back home, and I shall stay in this place only long enough to attend your ladyship's famous party.

" Said Lady Yellow-paw to my great, great, great, great, great, twenty-seven times great grandmother Pinky-white, when she had ended her story, said Lady Yellow-paw: 'Pinky-white, you do not speak of having a dog in your Happy Family.'

" She had hardly said this before a tittering, chuck-ling, clicking noise was heard and out spoke a pert little

I USED TO PLAY WITH A DOG'S TAIL!

spotted black-and-white kitten and said, 'Te! he! he! I used to play with a dog's tail! A black, peeked-nosed dog's tail, and his name was Trippy; and he was good to me. He had a curly tail.'

"'Silence!' cried the spotted black-and-white kitten's mother. 'Don't you know better than to speak up at a famous party — a little thing like you? Silence!'

"'Trippy liked me after you went away,' cried another

kitten; a white one. 'He liked me better than he liked
you. He let me play with his ears, and sleep on his
neck, and he cried for me when I
was out of his sight. When somebody threw me in the water, Trippy
took me out with his mouth.'

HE TOOK ME OUT.

"This kitten's mother was not at
the party, but its snappish old aunt,
Black Velvet, was there and she gave
it a smart box on the ear. 'It is a
pity,' said she, 'if at a famous party like this we
older ones cannot be heard for the noise of these
pert little minxes. I myself could tell a strange
story; a story stranger far than even the one just heard
from that very neat puss, Pinky-white, with her Happy
and her Unhappy, and her Not a Speck of Dirt! Was
she blown off a tree in a whirlwind? Answer me that; or
did she go to sea in a baby's crib? Answer me that.'

"Said Lady Yellow-paw to Black Velvet, 'Let me hear
your strange story, how you were blown off a tree in a
whirlwind, and how you came to go to sea in a baby's
crib.'

"Here the cat that hadn't common sense rushed
round the ring and stood on her head and said, 'I can

tell the strangest story of all, for I can tell why I haven't got common sense.'"

When the lovely Pussyanita had told thus far she stopped suddenly and said to King Grimalkum, "I beg your majesty's pardon. Oh King Grimalkum, you only wished to hear the story of my great, great, great, great, great, twenty-seven times great grandmother Pinky-white, and I have told, besides this, of the spotted black-and-white kitten who played with the peeked-nosed little black dog's tail, and of the white kitten he took out of the water, and have also spoken of Black Velvet who was blown off a tree in a whirlwind and afterwards went to sea in a baby's crib, and of the cat who hadn't common sense — I will say no more."

"You shall say more," said King Grimalkum, sternly. "I can never close my eyes to slumber until I know how it happened that Black Velvet was blown off a tree in a whirlwind and afterwards went to sea in a baby's crib.

"A baby's crib is a strange thing to go to sea in; why not in a boat? or in a tub? or even on a board? Why go to sea at all, when there is plenty of ground, and when cats hate water? And as for that other cat, why had she not common sense? She needed common sense. Every cat needs common sense."

" I can tell your majesty in a few words why the
cat that hadn't common sense hadn't common sense,"
replied Pussyanita. " It was because she lost it.
Do you ask how ? I answer by a looking-glass and a
clock.

"When quite young she looked in a looking-glass
and saw herself there, and thought it was another cat
staring at her, and got mad at that other cat, and flew at
it, and broke the glass, and frightened herself so that she
ran all over the house and when she came to the
clock the clock door was open and she jumped in. The
clock door got shut and she had long to stay there, and
the noises in the clock almost made her crazy, and she
never had common sense afterwards. This tells why the
cat that hadn't common sense hadn't common sense,"
continued Pussyanita ; "but to tell all about Black Velvet, and how it happened that she was blown off a tree in
a whirlwind, why she went to sea at all when there was
plenty of ground and cats hate water, will take a longer
time than I have to live."

" Time shall be granted you," cried King Grimalkum.
" Go on ! go on at once !"

The lovely Pussyanita then went on, and went on
at once, to tell the Story of Black Velvet as told by
herself at Lady Yellow-paw's famous party.

THE STORY OF BLACK VELVET.

" I was born in a barn. My brothers and sisters were born in the same place. There were four of us, all of the same age and size. As soon as we could run our mother took us all over the great barn-country.   She did every-thing for our good.   She showed us the holes and told us which were mouse holes and which were rat holes. She showed us how to spring and how to catch, and how to hold.   She brought us many kinds of eatable bugs and taught us to snap at flies and to beware of wasps. At night she went forth to hunt for us the slippery mole which slips so swiftly through the grass.   At day she purred us sweetly to sleep, or sometimes she let us go with her to the wheatfields and get a peep at the moles and watch the field mice running up and down the wheat stalks.

" We lived in the hayloft and oh what frolics we used

to have! What frolics! What frolics! We raced, we
scampered, we skipped, we hopped, we tumbled over each
other, we tumbled
over ourselves, we
chased each others'
tails, we chased our
own tails, we played
hide and seek in the
hay, we scrambled up
the beams, we ran
along the rafters, we
peeped down, we took
turns sitting in our
sunbeam — I speak

MOLES.

now of a sunbeam which shone through a knot-hole.

"Our mother liked to curl herself up and sit with her
eyes half shut watching our
sports. She would sit a long,
long time, scarcely moving,
except to stir the end of her tail.
We were happy to have her
near us. She was gentle in her
manners, though of course

WITH HER EYES HALF SHUT.

when she was watching, or catching, or holding, she looked
fierce. Any cat would do so. She was not one of the cross

kind, always cuffing and boxing and snapping and growling and spitting. She never punished us but once and that was when we were very little. We fell down the crooked stairs which led up to our home. She had always made us keep away from the small ends of the crooked stairs because there was no room there to put our paws.

WATCHING A MOUSE.

"One day our mother had been watching a mouse at the bottom of the crooked stairs while we played at the top. I hopped too near the small ends and peeped down and my brothers and sisters hopped at me, and down we all went, heels over head. Our mother was angry, for she lost the mouse. We went without our dinner and had other punishment which I need not mention.

WHITE SATIN AT HOME.

"Now the noise we made in falling down and in being punished was heard by some girls playing on the barn floor and they scrambled up a ladder to find out what was the matter. When one of the girls who climbed up the ladder saw me she said, 'Oh! oh! A black kitten! Do give it to me! She will make three! Then I shall have three black ones and three white ones!'

"'Yes! do take her!' said the other girl. 'If you don't take her she will be drowned.'

"The next day I was put in a box with holes in the cover and carried a long, long way to a strange place. This made me sorrowful, but still I was glad not to be drowned, and after the first day the five other kittens began to be friendly, and the two black ones were glad I came, for there were then as many black ones as white ones. I was named Black Velvet to match White Velvet. The others were Black Floss and White Floss and Black Satin and White Satin.

"White Satin used to run away and go home to her mother and her sisters. She had a gray mother and two gray sisters. Sometimes we went with her. She liked to play with her sisters and show them her ribbon. Our mistress wished us not to go and tried to keep us in the house. I did not like this, I wanted to scamper across the garden, or down to the river, or across a field to an

old barn.   I peeped all about and found good places to
get out by.   Then I used to coax White Velvet, and
White Floss, and White Satin, and Black Floss, and
Black Satin to go.   I always went first and they followed.

"There were two gray kittens living in the barn, and
the first day we went there these two ran and jumped into

THEY LOOKED DOWN UPON US.

a wheelbarrow and
looked down upon
us. Pretty soon they
began to stretch out
their necks, and
shake their tails.
Then they crept
down, then they
crept towards us, and
began to glare and
spit, and sputter, and
their tails grew so
big we thought we
had better go home.

"We liked to go
to the barn on ac-
count of the chances to catch mice.   The gray kittens flew
at us every time we went, and at last one of them hit White
Velvet in the eye and made it bleed.   Our mistress kept us

in the house after that, but we had fun racing over the beds and playing in the curtains. We played in the curtains so much that our claws had to be cut at the points. We were almost as well treated as children. Our milk was warmed, we had plenty of squash, and fish, and a good deal of chicken meat. Catnip was brought for us. We had each a basket to sleep in, and the baskets were trimmed with ribbons and had cushions. We had ribbons on our necks; the catnip was good.

"But I did not like staying in the house all the time and every chance there was I jumped out at an open window or door, and White Velvet, White Floss, White Satin, Black Floss and Black Satin all jumped and went wherever I went. But after the Great Whirlwind, I was kept in the house. I will now speak of the Great Whirlwind.

"It was a cold day and it seemed as if a door never would be left open, but one was left open at last, and out I went, and out went White Velvet, White Floss, White Satin, Black Floss and Black Satin after me. We raced across the fields to the barn. The gray kittens were not at home and we watched mouse holes, and chased mice till a man came and drove us out and shut the door tight.

"The wind blew; the sky was dark; the sun did not shine. We felt rain drops. This set us scampering. When we were in the field we saw a great dog coming and we ran to a tree and scampered up. I stopped to spit at the dog and was the last one up. The sky grew blacker, the wind blew harder and harder. The dog lay down on the ground and howled. Not one of us durst come down. The rain came hard upon us. The tree branches whirled round and round. It was a great wind. It was a whirlwind. It blew off all the leaves that had been left on and then it blew us off. For it was a great wind. Yes, a whirlwind. A dreadful whirlwind. I hope, dear Lady Yellow-paw, that neither you nor any one at this famous party will ever know the feeling of being blown off a tree in a whirlwind. I hope you nor any one at this famous party will know the feeling of being in a tree in a whirlwind with claws that have been pared down at the points. None of our bones were broken. How thankful we all ought to be that we are cats

WE SAW A GREAT DOG COMING.

and not children, for we have cushions on our feet, so that we can be blown down without having any bones broken.

" None of our bones were broken but we were drenched with the wet rain. We were almost dead with the fright and the wet rain and we crawled all the way home.

"Our mistress was looking for us. She said, 'Oh you naughties, come in quick!' We crawled in and she wiped us with a dry cloth and laid us in a row in front of the stove, and gave us a warm supper and then some catnip.

" After this she kept me in the house. Said she, 'Black Velvet, you put mischief into the others' heads and I will keep you in. Black Satin, Black Floss, White Velvet, White Floss and White Satin you may go. Black Velvet shall stay with me.'

" It was hard to see Black Floss, Black Satin, White Velvet, White Floss and White Satin skipping in the

OFF A TREE IN A WHIRLWIND.

yard, over fences, up and down clothes-poles, and be myself shut up indoors. But how little we know what is best for us! One day those others did of themselves go to a corn-house, and there they tasted bad meat which had been put there to kill rats, and they all died! Every one, Black Floss, Black Satin, White Velvet, White Floss, White Satin, every one died. Oh how my mistress did cry! And I too. Yes, I was sad and lonely. I went crying round from room to room, calling for my lost playmates. I looked in all their baskets.

"My mistress seemed to love me more than ever. 'I have only you, now, Black Velvet,' she would say. Then she would hug me and hug me. She let me do what I pleased. I had thick cream. When she was sewing I jumped on her shoulder and played in her hair, and I went to sleep in her hat, if I wanted to, and in her work-basket. When she went out to walk she used to take me with her and wrap me up in her apron, and talk to me. But when I grew to be a cat she made me a blanket of my own. It was a good one. It was my own blanket. She loved me a great deal.

"I said at the beginning of my story that it is wonderful story. You will say that this is true when you hear what happened to me next.

"One day the river grew very big and spread up to the

houses, yes, up over
the windows of the
houses, and broke
the houses in pieces.
I was sleeping in a
rocking chair and
the water wet me
and waked me from
sleep and I sprang
up on top the rock-
ing chair back, and
the water swashed
and there was a great
noise and the rock-
ing chair went sail-
ing off and many
other things went,
and the chair began
to go down deeper
and then I jumped
off on to a bucket.
Something hit that
a knock and I had
only time to catch

MY MISTRESS.

hold of a box; a small one. There was just room to get

all my paws on and I had to stick my back up high. I
expected every moment to be drowned.   I little
thought I should
live to tell the story.
But a piece of board
w a s   k n o c k e d
against m e .   I
sprang upon that.
Then came a chair.
I sprang upon that.
Then came some-
thing else ; some
thing wonderful,
but I said at the
beginning that this
is a w o n d e r f u l
story.   This next
thing was a baby's
crib with the baby
in it! The curtains
were open and the
baby was looking
out. I jumped from the chair to the cradle and lay down
on the baby. I was glad enough to get that resting place. I
felt safe with the baby.   Somebody would come to get

I FELT SAFE.

the baby. The baby put out its hands and took hold of me.

"I don't know what became of that poor baby. The crib tipped over. I heard a man speak, and perhaps he went and got the baby. I was lucky enough to jump on to a firkin, and on this I floated down, down, down, down, I don't know where, but I cried, cried, cried, oh how I cried!

"I bumped against something hard, something very big. I scrambled up. Men were on it, and a woman, and a girl, and boys. They clapped and shouted and laughed. Oh what a noise! Don't people know that loud noises make our ears ache? Don't they know that our ears are made to hear very little faint mouse-taps, butterfly-wing noises, and we can't bear loud noises? No, they don't know. But I must go on with my story.

"That big hard thing was not a house nor a barn. It moved over the water. You cats that have lived only on ground cannot think how dreadful it is to stay in the midst of water. Not a bit of ground! No grass to eat. Oh I thought I should die for want of a bit of something green! No trees to climb! But there were some very high poles set for me to climb; poles taller than trees, and ropes and everything handy fixed for me to hang on by. I was treated well. The men fed me, the women

fed me, the girl fed me, the boys fed me. The cook
taught me some tricks which I shall be happy to show
to those present at this famous party, if I shall be properly invited. A little girl held me and she put me around

her neck for a com-
forter. I let her do
it. The cook hung
a bell round my
neck. The noise of
it pained my ears,
and I was glad when
the woman took it
off. She took it off
because I used to
get into the place
where the girl slept,
and wake her up.

"Now when the
ship came to the
ground the cook put
me into a bag and
got into a cart. He

I USED TO GET INTO THE PLACE WHERE THE GIRL SLEPT.

was going to give me away. Pretty soon I smelled grass.
Then I scratched and cried. Oh how I did want a piece of
something green and to roll in the grass! Every cat here

knows it would be a hard thing to live without something green. I soon got something green, and plenty of it. The cook opened the bag a little, to show me to another man and I took a sudden spring and away I went, and the more he called, 'Puss! Puss! Puss!' the faster I ran, and at last I found myself all alone in the fields, in a strange country.

"I rolled over and over, and tore up the grass, and ran up and down trees, and then I lay down behind a bush and watched to see if there were any moles or field mice in that country. Pretty soon I saw two live things sitting together. They looked like rats, but they had white on them. They were sitting in the sun. I was going to spring at them, but I stopped. I was in a strange country. How did I know if the creatures were good to eat? They might be bad as that bad meat which killed

TWO LIVE THINGS SITTING TOGETHER.

poor White Velvet, White Satin, White Floss, Black

Satin, and Black Floss; or they might have dreadful teeth, or dreadful claws.

"While I was waiting a minute to think about it, I heard a sound in the grass; a creep, creep, creep, creeping sound in the grass. It was a cat. But she did not spring quick enough. They heard her and skipped out of sight quicker than a wink.

"As the cat sprang past me I could see that she had no tail. 'Poor thing,' I said, 'she has lost it in a trap!' Pretty soon I saw another cat without any tail. Then some kittens without any tails. I thought that must be a dreadful place for traps. I dared not step in the grass to hunt.

"I got very hungry keeping still without hunting for mice and moles, and at last I went to a house. In the yard of the house a black and white cat without a tail

THE BLACK AND WHITE CAT.

stood and looked at me.

"'What do you want here?' said she.

"'I want to go in the house,' said I.

"'Be off!' said she.

"'I won't!' said I.

"Then she began to spit, and she flew at me, and I flew at her. A woman

came running out and took me up. 'Oh you beautiful
creature!' she said. 'You've got a tail! I'm so glad to
get a cat with a tail.' I must tell you, dear Lady Yellow-
paw and all present at this famous party that the cats of
that strange place did not have any tails. 'No tails!'
cried Lady Yellow-paw and others. 'How then do they
show when they are glad and when they are mad?'

"I said at the beginning, dear Lady Yellow-paw, that
this is a wonderful story. Let me tell you that the
cats of that place do not wish to have tails. 'Not *wish*
to have tails?' cried Lady Yellow-paw and others at the
famous party. No, your ladyship. But let us not be
conceited and think our own ways are always the best.
To be sure a tail does add to the good looks of a cat,
still we all know that a tail *is* a great care; always likely
to get rocked on, or stepped on, or pulled, and is sometimes in the way when you want to sit down. That
no-tailed cat made my tail a way of hurting me. All
present must have seen that its tip is gone, though all
have been so polite as to seem not to notice this. It was
the doings of that jealous no-tailed cat. She was jealous
because so much notice was taken of me. She could not
bear me to come into the house. She clawed, and bit,
and spit at me so that my mistress had to let me sleep in
the room with herself and her little boy. One night I did

what pleased my mistress very much. One night a mouse jumped on her boy's bed, and waked him up, just as I used to wake up that girl when I had that bell on

my neck. I caught this mouse, and found him quite as good as any in our own country. My mistress praised me more than ever, after this, and held me, and stroked me a great deal, but her doing so made that other cat maul me worse than ever, and

THE MOUSE THAT BLACK VELVET CAUGHT.

I should have run away if my mistress herself had not come away. My mistress came to this country and brought me with her. Here I am, out of reach of that jealous cat's teeth and claws. Here I am well-fed and tended. Here I live an easy life. Yet still I am not happy. Would you know the reason why? My mistress has another cat, a partly white cat. People call her a beautiful cat. So she may be to any one who fancies white paws and white noses. I do not like to see my mistress hold that cat and stroke her. I am obliged to see it. I am obliged to see the boy like that

SOMETHING BLACK VELVET WAS NEVER, NEVER ALLOWED TO DO.

cat; hug that cat; I am even obliged to see her allowed
to jump up and eat milk from the same bowl with him,
something *I* have never been allowed to do!

"All this is hard to bear. I do not like to think about
it, and to keep myself from thinking about it I employ
myself in teaching the way of opening doors. Every cat
should know how to open doors. There may be times
in a cat's life when she may save her life by knowing
how to open a door. There are times in every cat's life
when she may get food by opening a door.

"Here a number of cats sprang to their feet and began
to tell of particular times when they had saved them-
selves and got food by knowing how to open doors.
Among them was the cat that hadn't common sense.
'One at a time, my dears,' said Lady Yellow-paw.
'Snowball, will you begin?'"

"But I humbly beg your Majesty's pardon," said the
lovely Pussyanita to the King. "The particular times
when all these saved themselves or got food by knowing
how to open doors were not in Black Velvet's story.
You asked, oh King, for Black Velvet's story. That is
ended, I am silent."

"You shall not be silent!" thundered King Grimalkum.
"Speak! As king of all the cats, I wish particularly to

know the particular times when all those saved themselves
and got food by knowing how to open doors.   As king of

SHE USED TO SIT ON A HIGH WALL.

all the cats, I should be well informed on all such matters."
   "To tell you what you ask," answered the lovely

Pussyanita, " would take a longer time than I have to live."

" Time shall be granted you," said the king. " Begin without delay to tell what Snowball told."

WHAT SNOWBALL TOLD.

"When my sister Lily and myself were quite young, but not very, the people who lived in the house began to talk of drowning us. Now all present at this famous party will agree with me that if we are to be drowned at all we should be drowned when we are too young to know anything about it. I suppose there is not one here present who would not rather have been drowned when she knew nothing about it, than to be drowned now.

"When our mother heard drowning spoken of she took us under the barn, and there we stayed a long time. We lived under the barn. Our mother would not let us come out. She used to sit on a high wall and we wanted to, but she said dogs would get us and boys would scare us. A small boy used to come out there with his books and his slates and his other things, and this small boy crawled under the barn and found us and dragged us out, and then our mother moved back to the house to live. On the very day we moved back, I was put into a covered basket and sent away in a rattling thing called a carriage. The noise it made frightened me almost to death. I scratched the basket and clawed the cover, and stuck my paws through, and mewed and cried, for I was dreadfully frightened at the rattling! At last they put me in a house. I was afraid to stay in that house. Everything in that house was strange to me. The people were strangers. It seemed like a dreadful place. The people put their own things on all the good high places, and every time I jumped on a good high place, there would be a running and a screaming enough to scare you out of your senses. As if kittens would knock things off! As if kittens were clumsy as people and could not walk *between*

JUST RIGHT TO SPRING AT.

things! You know kittens, and cats too, need high places to jump up to.

"There was a small boy in the house and he had a whip. I need say no more. You all know or can understand, what it is to live in the house with a boy and a whip. But I was going to say that even the oldest of us have been kittens once and we know that a kitten must spring at things a-moving. I did. The boy rode on a wooden horse, and the horse had a tail just right to spring at. It was placed behind the boy so that he could not see me. But the people could, and they punished me for doing what I could not help doing. A kitten would not be a kitten did it hold back from springing at such a beautiful tail a-moving.

"I was whipped and put down cellar a great many times and even when I had grown quite large; for I was always of a lively turn.

"Oh what fun I had with the people after I learned to open the cellar door! Mornings they would say ' I wonder who let the cat up?' Sometimes just after I had been put down cellar for meddling with tassels or knitting work, they would find me on the best bed or in the best chair, or in the best room curled up on the best

CURLED UP ON THE BEST RUG.

rug. At last these people took all their things and went away and left me there with nothing to eat. Every day

I had to go forth to seek my food.   Pinky-white has told you something of what this means.   Hanging around back doors, kicked, starved, frozen, barked at by dogs, chased by cruel boys!   Oh tongue cannot tell what I suffered from cruel boys!   They yelled at me, they threw stones, they tormented me in every way they could. Just the sight of one would make me tremble.   One day when I was on a clothes-pole I saw two boys coming, far away.   They yelled at me and picked up stones. I scrambled down.   I ran toward the house.   I heard their shouts.   I ran to the back door.   The door was shut.   I sprang up, caught the latch, the door opened, I ran in to a woman, looked in her face and said, 'Oh do take care of me!'

THE RAT FAMILY.

"The woman was so much pleased with my opening the door that she invited me to live in that house, and I was glad enough to stay for there is a meat-shop in the house.   I have lived there a very long time.   I make myself useful by driving off cats and dogs that come to steal meat. Of course I never steal. I do not need to. I am fed so well that I never know what it is to be hungry, and have no wish for mouse-meat or rat-meat. In fact the rats and I are such friends, I sit near them in the garret and watch their goings on in their families, and they never mind me at all.

" My good fortune came from knowing how to open doors. I will say no more, for I know the company wish to hear Madame Pussy Hunter's story.

MADAME PUSSY HUNTER'S STORY.

"I am chiefly an out-doors cat. I like to catch moles and field-mice and rabbits, and bugs, and butterflies. I like butterflies almost as well as Pussy Gray did. Poor Pussy Gray who was stung in the eye by a bumble-bee while watching for butterflies and went crazy! I am fond of birds too.

" In this I am different from the renowned Tabby Fur-purr, who found out a way of not liking birds, and on that account had her picture taken and put in a frame!

"I was always a butterfly hunter, but not always a mole hunter, a field mouse hunter and rabbit hunter. I will tell you how I happened to become a mole hunter, a field-mouse hunter, and a rabbit hunter.

"One day I went out among some tall flower-stalks to catch butterflies, and got very tired of jumping, and lay down to take a nap under the flower stalks. I was just dropping off to sleep when I heard a noise and looked up and saw my sister coming. She asked me to go to her house and get some cream. She knew where there was a good deal of cream in a good place. She wanted me to open the pantry door. As my sister was anxious for me to go, I went, and we both enjoyed a hearty meal. We crept out of the pantry and

JUST DROPPING OFF TO SLEEP.

THE DOG THAT WAS UPSIDE DOWN. 73

then softly under chairs and tables to the passage-way. In that passage-way was my sister's kitten playing with a ball of yarn. She pawed it, and clawed it, and pushed it, and tumbled heels over head over it, as kittens will do — ah, we were all kittens once! and at last she pushed it into a room. We peeped in at the door and saw the kitten leave the ball suddenly, and pop behind the screen. Her tail was very big, and her back was up, so we knew something had frightened her, and crept in to see what had frightened her. In the middle of the room was a great chair, and from that chair was something hanging down, something furry. We went near to see what it could be. It looked like a dog's head upside down. It *was* a dog's head upside down. Cats that have always seen dogs' heads upside up, have no idea how a dog's head looks upside down. This dog's head was upside down and the whole dog was upside down; upside down and asleep.

" Both our tails began to grow big. We left the room quickly, and softly as possible, and ran through a long passage, then up-stairs, then through another long passage, and *then* we heard the dog coming, barking! We ran faster. We knew he was on the stairs; knew he was after us. We got to the end of a long passage.

The bark of the dog sounded nearer and nearer. There was no way out of the passage. Oh what a moment that was! I saw a door. I sprang up twice, and opened it the second time trying. I tremble, even now, to think what might have become of us had not a window of that room been open, or had I not known how to open a door. We darted through that window, and went down by a water-spout. The dog looked out and turned and ran down-stairs, but by the time he was in the yard we were safe on a shed. Oh how thankful we ought to be that dogs cannot climb!

"I was saved, but in my haste I trod on a tack nail, and it stuck in my paw and made my paw in great pain. I went limping, and the pain of the paw made me sick. My dear mistress! How good she was to me! She took out the nail and bound up the sore place, and fed me with warm sweetened milk and water, or if I was thirsty, gave me cool, clear water to lap, and held me, and made for me a soft bed, and talked to me, and *poored* me. Oh how pleasant it is to be talked to and *poored!*

"I felt so grateful to my dear mistress that as soon as I was well I went out to catch everything I could for her — rabbits, moles, field-mice. That was why I became a hunter. Everything I could I brought in and laid at her feet, because I wanted to please her. I would not eat one of them until she told me I might.

I never ate even a mouse until I had shown it to her. Sometimes I bring birds. She is not pleased with me, then. She scolds me when I bring birds. I don't know why she scolds me for bringing birds. I should like to know the renowned Tabby Furpurr way of not liking birds.

"Scarcely had Madame Pussy Hunter finished when up sprang a Spry White Kitten and hopped out on three paws, and said: '*I* can tell a story of a door opening.' Some of the older ones tried to hiss her down. She was asked if her story would tell how she lost her right fore paw. Upon learning that her story would tell how she lost her right fore paw, they asked to hear what the Spry White Kitten had to say.

THE SPRY WHITE KITTEN'S STORY.

"It is a short story that I am going to tell, but I wish to tell it. I wish to say that for my part I have never

found any good come from
knowing how to open doors.
Not that I know how, but
my mother does. She opened
a door the other day to show
me some cream. It was but-
ter-cream streaming down a
butter-churn.   She told me
to jump up and lick, and I did, and a man
came and boxed
my ears and I have
not heard w e l l
since.

"An-
o t h e r
time to
p l e a s e
me, she
op e ned
a door
and let
me into a large din-
ng-room that had
long **curtains** just
right to scratch and

THE CAT WITH HER EARS TIED UP.

to climb up by, and a funny old feather hung over a funny old clock. I could go up on those good curtains, and jump to the clock and play with the feather. And one day I meddled with the clock to find out where its noise came from, and was caught and got the worst whipping I've ever had yet.

"Then here is my brother Bobby hiding yonder behind Black Velvet. Why does he hide? His ears are tied up with strings. Bobby likes work-baskets. He teased our mother to let him into a room where there was a work-basket. He played in it, and the girl tied his ears with strings, and he ran round, and rolled, and could not get them off, and ran into a coal-hole, and stayed till he was very hungry, and when he went into the house he went to a boy that was sitting on the floor eating milk. That boy did not give him any milk. No. He took a great cloth and tried to wash Bobby's paws in the milk! Bobby got away, and now he has come to this famous party with his ears in strings. A pretty state he is in to come to a famous party! We all know how dreadful it is to have our ears meddled with.

"But all this is nothing to what happened afterwards. My mother opened a door to let me into a room where there was a mouse-hole. Now a boy had put in that room a curious thing. I went close up to it to see what it was.

It was a crab, but I did not know that. I was young. I never had seen a crab. I touched it to find what it was made of, and it got hold of my leg just above my paw. I never screamed so in all my life. Oh how I did scream! And no wonder. My leg was broke. My paw had to be taken off, and now I have to be three-pawed. Now I have to go limp, limp, hopperty limp! Only three paws to run away from cruel boys with, and barking dogs! Only three paws to climb with! Only three paws to claw with! No; as for me, *I* have never seen much good come from knowing how to open doors!"

IT GOT HOLD OF MY LEG.

"'You had better sit down, Miss,' exclaimed Black Velvet. 'Young people should be seen and not heard. We are speaking at this famous party of the good of knowing how to open doors—not of the bad. Mrs. Beulah Black is present, and has something to relate which all will like to hear.'

MRS. BEULAH BLACK'S STORY.

"In me, my dear Lady Yellow-paw, you see a child of the unfortunate Pussy Gray who when watching for butterflies was stung in the eye by a bumble-bee and went crazy, and ran away. There were three of us born on the same day, namely: Lily, Dinah Dusky and myself, Beulah Black. Pussy Gray was one of the best of mothers. She herself cared neither for rats, mice, nor moles. She liked birds and bugs and was very fond of butterflies. But she would sit long watching at a hole to catch mice or moles for us, and then she would bring them to us, and show us how to play with them, and stand looking at us in her motherly way. She grew thin from staying in to take care of us. We were a quarrelsome set.

"I don't know what became of Lily, but Dinah Dusky went when she was very young to live in a corn store. I stayed at a house nearer my mother's house, and it was well that I did, for at the time she got stung in the eye by a bumble-bee, she had another young family, and I was able to go in and take care of them, and to punish them when they needed punishment. I was then a mother myself with my first little brood around me.

"I remember the day well. My mother left the family and went into the garden to catch butterflies. If she did not see any butterflies it was her custom to stand still and listen for the sound of their wings. She was doing so when that sad thing happened to her. My sister,

Dinah Dusky, had come that day to see my dear little
beauties and we two went out together to catch bugs for

them. Our mother was in the garden not far from us.
She stood stock still. She had heard the sound of a but-

terfly's wings. An instant more and she would have turned her head.

"Then it was that the bumble-bee stung her eye. She ran. We ran. We could not catch her. We could not think what made her behave so. She ran this way and that way, over fences, back again, through bushes, over bushes, across fields, and at last away she went out of sight and was never heard from afterwards. Every day my sister Dinah Dusky and I went forth to look for our mother, hoping to bring her home to her young family.

"It was when we had been in the fields looking for her that we saved ourselves by my sister's quickness in opening a door. I will explain how this happened.

"My sister and I went into a swamp to look for our mother, and we caught sight of a rabbit there. We lay down close to the ground, and crept, crept, crept, softly along, not making a bit of noise. Sometimes we stopped creeping; then we crept; then we stopped; then we crept, getting all the time nearer and nearer. The rabbit was asleep part way under a log. We had crept very near when all at once we heard the bark of a dog. Dreadful sound! In an instant we were on our feet and running. We ran towards a house. At first the dog did not see us. Then he saw us and ran after us, barking. Oh how frightened we were! We ran faster but he ran faster than we. He came near us, barking, barking, barking, oh it was terrible! For he came so close to me that I felt his breath. He caught me by the back of the neck, and just then a boy called him off, and he dropped me and went to the boy. I ran on. My sister had gone far ahead. We ran towards the back of the house. The dog came again. We heard him coming afar off. He would not stay with the boy. I almost died with fright. There wasn't a tree nor a clothes-pole near. But there

THE CAT THAT WAS STEALING MILK.

was a door that my sister had opened before at times when it was necessary that she should get something to eat without being seen. She opened this door now, and frightened a cat that was there stealing milk out of a pitcher, and made her tip over the pitcher.

"We went in and ran through a back shed to the barn. I sprang up on a hay rack, and my sister — all at this famous party will be surprised to hear what my sister did. My sister sprang up on the horse's back!

"We were not a minute too quick. We just saved ourselves. The dog was close behind. But he could not get at us and he had to go away.

"I have more to tell. That horse and my sister became friends. When he stayed in the barn she used to stay on his back. He liked to have her stay there. He could not bear to be without her. He was not easy unless she came and stayed on his back.

"The man said it would not do. He said it would hurt the horse and they carried him far away.

"Now comes the sorrowful part. My sister mourned so for the horse that she would not eat. She would only lap a little water sometimes. She grew weak and thin. She did not clean her fur. She would stay in the barn and lie down on the spot where the horse used to stand. At last she was seen no more and after a long time she was found, dead, high up on a hay-mow in a far corner!

"This is all I have to say, your ladyship, but my

MY SISTER SPRANG UP ON THE HORSE'S BACK!

younger brother David is here. Though now bigger **than** I, he was once smaller. He was one of the young kittens our mother left when she went out to catch butterflies and was stung in the eye by a bumble-bee. David will tell you of a time when he opened a door and ran away, and why he ran away."

All present said they would like to hear David's Story, and he began as follows:

DAVID'S STORY.

" I was one of the young kittens Pussy Gray left when she went out to catch butterflies. My sister Beulah Black has told you what happened to Pussy Gray, how she went crazy and went nobody knew where, and was never heard from afterwards.

"My Sister Beulah Black had a young family of her own, and one day she tried to carry us to her house, in order that she might not have to be all the time running back and forth. It happened that I dropped into a hole,

and she could not get me out. She had to leave me.
Now this was lucky for me, for the others of my mother's
young family, and all but one of my sister Beulah
Black's young family were sent away and lost. I have
often wondered why it is that so many little kittens are
sent away and lost.

"Only for falling in that hole I might not be here. But
I came near dying there. When taken out I was almost
starved to death. I could not move; I could not make a
sound. Girl-Nellie took me out and kept me for her
own. She made me a cotton-wool bed in a cricket, she
covered me over
with silk, she fed
me with a spoon,
she held me just
as if I had been a
baby. And when
I grew larger she
used to rock me
in the baby's cra-
dle and sing to me.
She took turns
rocking me and

SHE TOOK TURNS ROCKING ME AND HER DOLLY.

her dolly, and when dolly was being rocked I sat
and waited for my turn to be rocked and sung

to. Oh, how I did love **my** little mistress! I wanted to
sit on her lap. I wanted to be with her a great deal. I
told her all this, though perhaps she never understood
what I said. I knew the time for her to come home
from school, and went always to meet her. She did not
know how I knew the time. People do not know how
cats know things. My dear mistress would not let boy-
John torment me. Boy-John was not cruel, but he
wished me to sit up on my hind legs, and to hold a
stick, and to jump through a hoop. It was easy enough
to do such things but I
did not like to do them.
Boy-John used to say to
the baby, 'Come Baby,
bring David!' I was so
big then that baby could
hardly lift me, but he
would drag me, and push
me, and try to lift me.

"Many at this fa-
mous party have spoken
of what they have suf-

COULD HARDLY LIFT ME.

fered from cruel boys and from dogs, but nobody
as yet has spoken of a baby. Tongue cannot tell what
I suffered from that baby. A baby will step on any part

of a cat. A baby will sit on a cat. A baby does **not** mind what part of a cat it lifts up a cat by, whether by the tail or by a leg, or by the head. A baby will pull your ears, will stick its finger in your eyes, will even meddle with your smellers, and you must keep from touching it, because it is a baby.

" I never did touch that baby to hurt it. I loved that baby. I kept my claws way in out of sight, and if I ever squealed it was sometimes when he sat down on me hard, and squelched the squeal out of me before I knew it.

" I come now to something painful to speak of. You will be surprised to learn that I ran away from that dear Nellie mistress. This will now be explained.

" Unhappily for me, I had great skill in charming birds, and I was as fond of birds as my mother Pussy Gray was of butterflies. I mean I was fond of them as food, not as friends. There was no cat anywhere around that could charm a bird as well as I could. I used to stay under a tree and when a bird came and sat on a bough I would look straight up at him, and then he could not fly away. He would cry, and flutter his wings, but he could not fly away. He would have to drop.

" I **used** to **carry** the birds to my dear mistress, for

I DROPPED THE BIRD.

I wanted to please her, and birds were the best things I could get. But she was not pleased; she scolded me. I could not understand why she praised me for catching a mouse and scolded me for catching a bird. A bird is better than a mouse. Pretty soon she began to do something besides to scold. I was punished in the way cats are punished. I need not tell. All at this famous party know. After I had been punished a great deal I kept away from trees. But one day I was in a window-seat, asleep. The window was swung open, and I lay there to enjoy the sunshine and fell asleep. The noise of a bird woke me. I stretched myself out flat and looked up. The bird was on a high window above. When I had looked at it a little while it began to cry, and then it flew down to the top of the window that was swung open. It flew lower and lower, and I made a spring and caught it. My mistress came in and I dropped the bird on the window-seat, and jumped down and crept away. I felt so ashamed I did not know what to do.

I was not whipped, but I was punished. I punished myself. I left that pleasant home and my dear mistress. You will understand why when I explain.

"That night my mistress' mother said, 'We cannot have David killing so many birds. Something must be done with him. I will get a boy to do something with him early in the morning.' I knew what she said. I did not know by the way people know. I knew by the cat-way of knowing, and not by the people-way. All present at this famous party know how cats know what people say. I understood what my mistress said, but I kept still under a table, and when nobody was looking I crept under the chairs out into the back room, and opened two doors and ran away, far away, and for a long time I lived the dreadful life of a cat without a home.

"One day a man invited me to go home with him. He keeps a store. There are herring and eggs in the store. I have lived there quite a long time. I want to go back to my dear mistress, but I am afraid they will get a boy to do something with me. I like to suck eggs, though as my master keeps a stick I do not take any except the broken ones he gives me. When I tease for herring he gives me a piece. I watch people and if they touch anything that belongs to my master I lay my paw on them and speak.

"Scarcely had David finished when out popped two gray little kittens, twins, both named Kittywinks, saying:

"'We are the Kittywinkses, and we've come to this famous party.'

"Lady Yellow-paw waved her paw and said: 'One Kittywinks at a time, my dears.'

THE GOOD CHILD-BABY.   99

"One Kittywinks then said: 'David talked about a child-baby. Call bad. Child-baby not bad. We've got a child-baby. He does not step on us. He does not sit down on us. He does not squelch us. He does not hurt. He touches us softly. He would *never* tie strings on our ears. He poors us, and strokes us, and lets us sit on chairs and sofas with him, and crawl all over him, and play with his curls, and play with his beads, and play with his playthings. He likes us, only he does not like to have us kiss him with our noses, but with our mouths, but we don't know how to kiss with our mouths, and we have to kiss with our noses.'

"And the Kittywinkses capered back to their places.

"All present at Lady Yellow-paw's famous party were pleased with the Kittywinkses, and no wonder, for they were a merry pair of twins, and not much like the sour faced ones, Tweedledum and Tweedledee, called in the story, *Dum* and *Dee*."

"What story?" cried King Grimalkum in a stern voice.

"The story of the renowned Tabby Furpurr," answered the lovely Pussyanita. "Tabby Furpurr who found out a way of not liking birds, and had her picture taken and set in a frame."

"I wish to hear the story," cried the King. "Tell it."

"With pleasure, your majesty," replied the lovely Pussyanita, "but to do so will take a longer time than I have to live."

"Time shall be granted you," answered the king. "Tell all you ever heard of Tweedledum and Tweedledee, and of the renowned Tabby Furpurr."

The lovely Pussyanita bowed and began to tell all she had ever heard of Tweedledum and Tweedledee and of the renowned Tabby Furpurr.

TWEEDLEDUM AND TWEEDLEDEE.

" In the days when Mouseroun al Ratchid was King of all the Cats, it was his custom to disguise himself in mealbag powder and walk about the country to see what he could see, and see it without being known.

" One cloudy morning soon before a storm — the time when our race are liveliest — Mouseroun called Phi, his wisdom cat, and the two set forth upon their travels. After proceeding quite a distance they came in sight of a small boy with a porridge pot, sitting under a tree, eating porridge.   A white cat close to his feet begged for the

THE GOOD-KIND BOY.

porridge, and a big dog stood by and licked the boy's face and begged for porridge, and put his nose in the boy's bread-bag.

"'Of what kind is the boy?' asked Mouseroun of Phi.

"'Of the good kind,' replied Phi.

"'How knowest thou that, oh Phi?'

"'Because the dog and cat come close and show no fear. They ask for food, sure of getting it.'

"'Tell me, oh learned Phi, why a boy has long claws only on his fore legs.'

"'Because his hind legs are for walking and standing,' replied Phi; 'and for walking and standing, short claws are better than long claws.'

"'Tell me further,' inquired Mouseroun, 'why a cat mews and a dog barks.'

"'For the same reason that a cow moos and a horse neighs, and a pig squeals, and a bird sings, and a frog croaks, and people speak,' answered Phi. 'Of course all these would mew if they could, but as they cannot mew they must do what they can do.'

"'And why, oh Phi, are some cats born white, and others black, and others gray, and others of divers colors?'

"'Because,' answered Phi, 'it takes all kinds of cats to make a world.'

"Just at this moment a young black and white cat came up and began spitting at the dog, and clawing the cat, and biting the boy's toes. When the dog growled, the cross cat ran out of sight.

"'Shall we go on and observe what that ill behaved creature will do next?' asked Phi.

"'By all means,' answered Mouseroun, 'but look where at yonder window a ribboned white cat sits stiff and straight, gazing at something afar. Let us hasten thither.'

"They hastened, and when they reached the window Mouseroun asked of the ribboned white cat: 'Oh, ribboned white cat, sitting stiff and straight gazing at something afar, at what art thou gazing, and what is thy name?'

"'I am gazing at flies,' answered the rib-

CUPEP THE CAREFUL.

boned white cat, 'and I am called Cupep the Careful.'

"Mouseroun made a sign to Phi to ask of the ribboned white cat why he was called Cupep the Careful. Phi did so.

"'Because I can be trusted,' replied the ribboned white cat to Phi, 'and trusted in any place, among china, glass, pictures, bottles, papers, no matter how high the shelf, how narrow, or how full. I step in and out so carefully that no harm is ever done. Nobody minds even if I step on the baby's face. You see I am allowed here with papers and a bottle and feather, easy to upset. All this is why I am called Cupep the Careful. I shall presently sit on the paper, and to sit on paper is pleasant.'

"As Cupep the Careful finished telling why he was called Cupep the Careful, Mouseroun drew Phi's attention to two dark objects sitting in a barn at some distance. Bidding Cupep the Careful good morning they went towards the barn and found that the two dark objects were two black and white young cats. Said Phi, 'These must be the sour faced twins, Tweedledum and Tweedledee, called *Dum* and *Dee*. I have often heard of them, but never any good.'

TWEEDLEDUM AND TWEEDLEDEE.

"They went nearer. The sour faced twins sat side by side looking cross and unhappy. Mouseroun motioned to Phi to address them.

" 'Are you not the twins Tweedledum and Tweedledee, called *Dum* and *Dee?*' asked Phi, 'and is it not one of you which shortly ago bit the toes of a boy, and spit at his dog, and clawed his cat?'

" 'It was I,' said Tweedledee, ' who did that. I could not maul Cupep the Careful and I meant to maul somebody. I will maul him if I can. The stuck-up thing! Everybody praises him. He has a watch to wear. Nobody praises me and I have not even a ribbon. He has had his picture taken and hung up. Why don't they take my picture?'

" ' They'd much better take mine,' snarled Tweedledum. ' I've been crying to have my picture taken ever since I saw that one of Tabby Fur-purr who found out a way of not liking birds, and on that account had her picture taken and set in a pussy willow frame. They won't take my picture. But I'll be even with them. I get hold of the clock strings, I tangle yarn, I won't purr, I climb posts and tear down the flowers, I scratch the baby's face, I pull away his playthings, I wait on the doorstep and bite his fingers,

I BITE THE BABY'S FINGERS.

when he tries to reach me, and I kill birds. *I'm* not going to find a way of not liking birds if they won't have my picture taken! I am better looking than Tabby Furpurr; I'm sweet and lovely.'

"'I am sweet and lovely myself,' said *Dee.*

"'You're not!' said *Dum.*

"'I am?' said *Dee.*

"'Say it again!' said *Dum.*

"'I do say it again!' said *Dee.*

"'Take that!' said *Dum.*

"'Take that!' said Dee. And the two seemed as if they would tear each other's eyes out, so that Mouseroun was wroth, and Phi had much ado to keep him from punishing them both on the spot.

"'A future time is better,' said Phi. 'To act in anger is to make ourselves like these. Come, let us go and seek out the much renowned Tabby Furpurr who found out a way of not liking birds, and who on that account had her picture taken and set in a pussy-willow frame.

"Mouseroun and Phi pursued their journey, rambling hither and thither, listening to the speech of bees, flies, bugs, worms, toads and frogs, and to the butterflies' happy hum, which is too faint to be heard by the clumsy ears of people — people who think they hear everything and hear so little!

" ' Dost thou know,' asked Mouseroun at last, ' where dwelleth this renowned Tabby Furpurr?'

" ' I have not that knowledge,' replied Phi.   ' She must

TABBY FURPURR.

be now quite aged, and therefore well known hereabouts. Yonder is a young Persian, all so happy with her three kittens, as soft and white as herself.   I will inquire of her concerning Tabby Furpurr. As they approached the young Persian, Phi inquired of her, 'Dost thou know Mistress Tabby Furpurr, young Persian, and canst thou direct us to her abode?'

"'I know Mistress Furpurr well enough,' said the young Persian, 'but I decline to direct you to her abode. It is too much trouble.'

"'We are anxious to find her,' said Phi, 'and we are weary with travel.'

"'No doubt,' replied the Persian; 'but I prefer to stay and enjoy the company of my children.'

THE HAPPY YOUNG PERSIAN.

"'And wilt thou not direct us?' asked Phi.

"Answered the young Persian, 'I have said what I have said.'

"'Good day, then,' said Phi, and he drew Mouscroun away, fearing he might do something rash.

"'Canst thou explain,' asked Mouseroun of Phi as they journeyed on, 'why the young Persian should refuse to please others when she is herself so happy?'

"'The most happy are often the most selfish,' replied Phi. 'Those who have known unhappiness are likely to feel pity.'

"A little farther on they looked in at a great stone doorway and there they spied a rat which had hidden in a dark corner to eat a head of wheat. 'Rats are wise,' said Phi, 'perhaps yon-der fellow may direct us to Mistress Tabby Furpurr.'

THE RAT.

"But as they drew near to inquire of the rat, he dropped his wheat and fled.

"'Now, why was that?' asked Mous-eroun. 'We meant him no harm.'

"'A rat,' said Phi, 'must judge by what has been done, not by what is meant. After all that has been done by cats to rats, it will take a long time to make rats believe that cats mean rats no harm.

"'I fear we shall not get any rat to direct us to the abode of Mistress Furpurr.'

TAKEN IN A TRAP.

"Phi was mistaken. Soon after, in passing a barn they heard much stir and scampering inside. 'Wherever there is a stir and a scampering,' said Phi, 'we may be sure there is something going on inside.'

"Mouseroun was eager to enter, but Phi held him back lest harm might befall him and himself stepped forward.

"'Rats,' he whispered, as he stepped back.

"There were six rats inside the barn; a father, mother and four children had come to visit

one of the family that had been taken in a trap. The
mother looked in at the front of the cage, the father
looked down from over the top. As Mouseroun and
Phi drew near, the father, mother and four children fled
to their holes.

"The rat in the cage when questioned by Phi, said he
had been told by his parents not to go in, but he thought
he knew best, and he did not believe the trap would shut
down so quick.

"Did he know where Mistress Tabby Furpurr lived?
and would he tell?

"Oh yes, he had reasons for knowing where Mistress
Tabby Furpurr lived, and he would tell, and he did tell
and with a kind good day, Mouseroun and Phi passed on
their way.

"'I observed,' said Mouseroun to Phi, as they passed
on their way, 'that the rat in the trap showed no fear of
us. How was that?'

"'It must have been,' said Phi, 'that he knew we could
not get at him.'

"'True,' said Mouseroun. 'Thou art truly a Cat of
Wisdom.'

"Not very long after this, Mouseroun and Phi reached
the abode of the renowned Tabby Furpurr and heard the
story of her life.

WE WENT BACK.

STORY OF MISTRESS TABBY FURPURR.

"I was one of two kittens born in a respectable corner of a garret. My twin sister was sickly and died at an early age, and my mother, being lonely, stole a black kitten from another cat. The black kitten's mother came to get her, but my mother was big and strong and with the help of my two older sisters she drove away the black kitten's mother and kept the black kitten.

THE BLACK KITTEN.

"I did not like that black kitten. She was coarse-haired, she bit my tail, and when I had spools, or marbles. or knitting-work to play with, she got them away from me.

"One day when she bit my tail I flew at her throat and gave it a bad bite and made it bleed. I never saw her after-wards. I did not know what became of her but I never saw her afterwards, except in dreams. I had dreadful dreams.   Once I dreamed I saw her sitting over the fireplace, holding her paw to her throat, and next time I

FIRST DREAM.

dreamed she came close to me with her mouth and eyes wide open and glared at me.

" My older sisters grew so large that the people thought they would send me and my mother away. They got us into a basket, and shut down the covers quick, and carried us very far. They thought my mother would never find the way back.   My mother did.   We got home at night, but my mother climbed up to the house top with me in her mouth and jumped through a window that she knew in the roof and in the morning they found us on the rug.

"Not long after this my mother was shot for her beautiful skin.   I was so lonely that I mourned very much.   The dog took care of me.   I did not think Nep would be so kind,

SECOND DREAM.

for sometimes he had barked at me but when he knew I was sorry and lonesome he asked me to snuggle close to him and if any people touched me he drove them away.

"SCAMPER UP AND DOWN HIS BIG SIDES AND TICKLE HIS PAWS, AND HIS NOSE."

"When my older sisters saw me with Nep they
wanted to come and he let them cmoe. We warmed our
feet in his hair. My sisters were too lazy to play, but one
of them used to catch fleas in his
hair. I did not like to catch fleas.
I liked to scamper up and down his
big sides and tickle his paws, and
his nose. He used to give me some
of his meat. He did not give my
sisters any. I will now explain
why I left Nep and that house.

"A pretty-faced white kitten used to come and play
with me sometimes. One day when I was asleep on the
door-mat, I was waked by a small noise and there was
the white kitten's face looking in at the door. She
wanted me to go and see two rats. She said two rats
went every day to a place to sit in the sun and we could
stay behind a rock and peep at them.

"I went with her to see the rats. They were too big
for us to meddle with, but we could peep at them.

"The white kitten liked to frolic and we raced
over the fields and on the fences as much as we
wanted to.

"All at once we heard a noise. People came. The
white kitten got away but a man caught me, and

carried me in some whistling cars to his home. He wanted to keep me. I was afraid to stay in that strange place and I squeezed out through a hole in the cellar.

THE TWO RATS IN THE SUN.

"Then something dreadful happened. I was chased by boys. They were dreadful boys. They hurt me. They made me tremble. They did things too cruel to mention.

"They set a dog on me. I could hardly move, I trembled so. I crept under a rail and the dog stayed there, barking I thought he would seize me, but before he did it a boy came and took me and treated me kindly, and carried me in his arms to his own home and took care of me.

"Oh how I did love that boy! I wanted to stay with him all the time.

"Every day when he went to school he let me go with him as far as the bridge.

"Then I would look up in his face and mew, 'Mayn't I go further?'

"He would lift up his finger and say, 'No, Tabby Furpurr. Go back!' And I always went back. But when it was time for him to come home I went to the bridge and

THE BOY THAT TREATED ME KINDLY.

HE NIBBLES THE PINK.

waited till he came and then went to the house with him. The boy's dog did not like to have the boy like me so much. He was not so good as Nep. He would not let me warm my feet in his hair. He looked at me when I stole cream or custard. If they caught me stealing cream or custard, I hung my tail and went over to the grandma house to stay. When grandma caught me stealing I hung my tail and went back to the boy's house to stay. A girl lived in the boy's house, and she tamed a mouse. It stayed in a box. One day the boy looked at me hard, and lifted up his finger and said, Tabby Furpurr, you have had enough to eat. This mouse is not for you. I am

going to let this mouse out. Don't you touch **this** mouse. Do you hear? *Don't you touch it!*'

"I knew what he said, and I never did touch that mouse. The girl played with it and let it stay in her work basket. It liked to nibble green things that were brought into the house.

"One day it got at a flower that the girl put in water and hung up, and it nibbled the flower. One day it was nibbling something green and it knocked over the thing the green was in and spilt the water on me and scared me, and made me jump, though I was quite an old cat then, and could not jump as spry as a kitten.

"It was at this time that I had my fight with a woods cat. She came to our barn. I never saw her before. I went to the barn to get some catnip. There was catnip among the hay, and when I felt that I needed catnip I went and picked it out of the hay. That woods cat came to get some of the catnip, but she had no right there. It was in a place under the haymow and a great deal of the catnip hay was there. The woods cat was sitting on it, pawing it with her paw.

"She flew at me, and we had a fight. She would have killed me if the girl had not come with a broom.

"I was a bad looking cat. I went lame and had salve on me. The girl took care of me, and as soon as I could walk she let me go in the garden with her when she picked flowers. I liked to go into the garden. She used to sit under a tree and read a book, and I used to sit on the seat close to her, and if she stroked me I purred loud.

"But she found out I liked birds. She saw me under a currant-bush eating a bird, and whipped me with a stick and said, 'Shame, Tabby Furpurr! Shame on you to eat a little bird?' And I went to the grandma house to stay.

" A bird came to live in our house. It lived in a cage
high on the wall. The boy showed me the bird and
looked at me hard, and lifted up his finger and said, ' Tabby
Furpurr, don't you touch that bird. That bird is not for
you. *Don't you touch that bird!*'

" I did not mean to do anything to that bird. But it
kept moving and hopping, and shaking its wings, and
shaking its tail, and it made me look at it ; and one day
when it shook itself very much I looked at it a long time
and at last I jumped at it. Before I knew what I was
going to do I jumped at it, and the cage fell down. I
could not get the bird. He kept himself in a corner.

" The boy's dog barked and ran to tell the people something was the matter, and they all came and spoke loud
and held up their fingers and cried 'Shame! Shame!'

" I went over to the grandma house and hid under a bed
and stayed till I was almost starved. Then I crawled out
and put my paw on grandma's foot, and looked up in her
face and she gave me some milk, and let me warm me at
her fire.

" Something happened to her duck. It let its little ducks
go with it under the bridge to the pond, and it got
itself killed. There was a rat there, and it was going to
get one of her little ducks, and she began to fight the rat,
and the mother rat came out and helped fight the duck,

and the boy drove them away, but afterwards the duck
died and left the little ducks.

" But grandma had a barn cat. She was not a Tabby.
She was only a black and white cat, but she was a very
good cat. She never would touch a bird or a chicken,
and she never would suck an egg. She did not like me.
She would not let me come in her barn. I did not let her
come in my barn. She was a good cat for not liking
birds.

" The boy carried the little ducks to the barn and tried
to make a hen that was there take care of them. She
would not do that. She went and left them. She would
not scratch up worms for them. The other ducks would
not. They had to take care of their own children, and
these little ducks stayed all alone by themselves, and cried
for their mother.

" Now that barn cat, though she was only a black and
white cat and not a Tabby, sat down there with the little
ducks and took care of them. Every day she went there
and stayed with the ducks, and when they went into a
puddle she mewed for them to come back.

" When she sat taking care of the little ducks, people
used to come and look at her. The first time she took
care of them grandma's dog barked at her. When
grandma told him it was all right, and let him see her

stroke the barn cat, he went away, but sometimes he came to look at that cat and the ducks to see if all was right. Sometimes the cat would spit at him. She would spit at anybody that touched one of her little ducks. When the little ducks went in wet places she took them by their necks and brought them out, and she carried them by their necks so much that they had crooked necks. One day a strange cat, a great white Tommy, came and looked in at the barn door when she was staying with the little ducks and she flew at him quick, and almost clawed his eyes out and he was glad to run.

"One day I wanted very much to taste of a little duck and I tried to get one, and I hurt its leg, and she clawed me and made me drop it, and grandma shamed me and I went back to the boy's house and hid under a bed, and when I was almost starved I crawled out and the boy whipped me hard and carried me back to the grandma house, and into her barn, and showed me that barn cat with the little ducks, and lifted

THE DUCK'S DEFENDER.

up his finger, and looked at me hard, and whipped me
again and said: 'Tabby Furpurr, don't you see that
barn cat staying with ducks and not eating any? And
you even fly at birds! Don't you ever touch any kind of
bird again. Do you hear? Find out a way of not liking
birds. *Find out a way of not liking birds! Remember!'*

"I knew what he said, though not in the way people
know. I knew by the cat way. I remembered by the
cat way of remembering. I
kept very still, I did not steal,
and when they thought I was
asleep I was finding out a
way of not liking birds, and
after I found it out I never
touched a bird again, nor a
duck, nor a chicken. I stayed
with the girl under the tree
and never touched a bird. I
watched the bird in the cage

THEY THOUGHT I WAS ASLEEP.

when he hopped and shook his tail and did not jump at
him, and I would not let any other cat touch a bird
nor a duck nor a chicken.

" One day when some killed chickens were hanging up,
a great Maltese cat came and looked at them and was
going to jump for them but I spit at her and drove her

away.   The people were pleased with me all the time and
the girl let me stay in the room when the bird's cage-door

was open and when he flew out; and
more birds came there to live and
the birds had little birds, and they grew
big birds, and I was a friend to them,
and the girl got a very big cage for all
the birds and sometimes she let me
stay in there with them and I did not
touch one.   They would stand on my
head and walk on my fur, and I let
them.   The boy was pleased with me
and the girl was pleased with me.

"I am an old cat now; a very old
cat.   I do not care for balls, or
spools, or marbles, or knitting-
work, or tassels, or strings.   I
do not wish to jump high.   I

GOING TO JUMP FOR THEM.

like to sit by the fire and feel the *warm* all around me.
You have heard my story!

"Mouseroun made a sign to Phi by which Phi understood that Mouseroun wished him to ask Mistress
Tabby Furpurr the way she found out of not liking
birds.

"'Excuse me to-day,' replied Mistress Tabby Furpurr

to Phi's question. 'I am weary and must take my repose. Some other time I will tell.'

"Soon after this Mouseroun and Phi went to a great Battle of the Cats and were long absent. Upon their return they set forth as before to travel about the country, and again sought out the abode of Mistress Tabby Fur- purr.

"As they journeyed on they were met by two lively young black and white cats, the same two they met before, Tweedledum and Tweedledee, called *Dum* and *Dee*.

"They were full of frolic and good-nature, tumbling over each other, and snatching at each other's tails.

"'Whither so fast?' asked Phi of them as they met.

" 'To catch some bugs for a cat with a large family of kittens,' they said.

"You are not as sour as you were," said Phi.

" 'Oh, no,' said *Dum* and *Dee*. 'It is folly to be sour when sweet is better. We found that out.'

" 'You might have your pictures taken now,' said Phi.

" 'We're so happy we don't care to,' said *Dum* and *Dee*. 'Good day to you.'

" 'Beware of guns,' said a faint voice near by.

"It was the faint voice of a feeble cat who had crept under a bush to die.

" 'We're not afraid,' said *Dum* and *Dee*. 'We have our nine lives, you know.'

" 'Go not quickly through them as I have done,' said the feeble cat. 'Beware of dogs, beware of stones, beware of guns, beware of shutting up, beware of boys, beware of drowning, beware of hot water, beware of stepping on, beware of wet blacking-brushes.'

" ' I have lived eight lives, and am now dying of a spot of blacking.'

" 'Tell us about the eight lives,' said *Dum* and *Dee*; and at a sign from Mouscroun, Phi made the same request.

" ' I will try,' replied the feeble cat, 'if you will bear with my weakness.'

THE STORY OF THE FEEBLE CAT AND HER NINE LIVES.

" My name is Pixie. I have lived my eight lives, speaking after the manner of cats, and am now in my ninth, which will soon end.

" When I was small and very young I was dropped in water. The water washed me back to the sand. I could not stir. I was kicked. People said 'dead kitten.' A great cat took me to a good place and licked me, and I opened my eyes. The great cat came many times. I should not have lived if she had not caught butterflies and grasshoppers for me. She got very good butterflies. Sometimes her spotted kitten came to see me, and some

times she went to the fields with her mother to get butterflies and grasshoppers for me, and one day she brought

me a very big grass-
hopper.

"When I could
stand on all my feet
the great cat carried
me in her mouth to
a house and a girl
let me come in, and

TO CATCH BUTTERFLIES.

I was that girl's kitten. She held me a great deal. Once
when I was crawling on the floor, the boy walked across

and he stepped on
me so hard that I
was all out flat, and
they took me up on
a shovel and car-
ried me out to
another room to
stay till I could
be buried. Next
morning the girl
came out there cry-
ing because her
kitten was dead.

SHE BROUGHT ME A VERY BIG GRASSHOPPER.

The boy came with a shovel to bury

I WAS SCARED.

PALMER COX.

143

me; but I was crawling on the hearth. The boy said,
'Hurrah for Pixie!' and the girl hugged me and kissed
me.

"One day the boy took something off the stove, and tied
the dog to it and told the girl to carry me to ride; and
she put me in and tried to carry me to ride, but it was
too warm, and I was scared of riding in it, and jumped
out and ran with all my might through the house and up-
stairs, and hid in a closet. The closet-door got shut and I
stayed there. I had nothing to eat. I mewed all the
time, but the people were far away. When I could not
mew any longer I dropped down. There was nothing left
of me but my skin and my bones. When the people
found me they took me out-doors to bury me. They put
me in the sunshine and in a little while I opened my eyes.
I was close to the hens' clams, and I ate some and crawled
away from that place, and the boy carried me into the
house, and I got well.

"Mornings I scratched on the girl's door and when I
was let in I jumped upon her bed and played with her
nose and with her toes, and sat on her and purred loud.

" A white cat lived in that house. She was not my
girl's cat. She was the small girl's cat. She could not
purr. She had no voice to purr. The small girl put
the white cat's ear close to my mouth and said, 'Pur;

like Pixie!' and the boy rubbed her paws together, to make her purr, and squeezed her tail softly and stroked her, but she did not purr. She had no voice to purr.

" The white cat and I played together with the balls and the spools and the hammock strings and the knitting work, and sometimes Pomp, the dog, played with us. The

dog liked to play. When the small girl stayed in the hammock to sew her work and see picture books, the white cat used to stay in the hammock or close by, and take a nap ; but the boy used to come and make her jump, and sometimes Pomp came there and jumped in the hammock.

"When the white cat grew older she had some kittens. I had not had any kittens. She was taken much notice of. The white cat lost all her kittens but one and as soon as that one could run she and her mother were sent away. Then the small girl held me and I was glad, for she spoke to me softly and touched me softly. She liked me because I could purr.

"One morning the white cat came back with her kitten. I saw her standing at the door to be let in, and I knew she ought not to come back, and I tried to drive her away, and we had a fight, and a cruel woman threw hot water at us from the kitchen, and it scalded my head and I went under some bushes to die. I could not see; I went by my smellers. When people found me they called me but I would not come out. They brought me some milk and a piece of meat, and I ate a little, and when I could see with both eyes I came out, but my neck has always been stiff on one side.

"The next time I almost got killed it was by a heavy stone. The stone fell on me. I liked to go in the garden and climb upon a high wall and see what was on the other side. A Molly girl lived on the other side, and a horse, and a dog, and two great cats, and hens, and there was a great deal there that was good to eat. The Molly girl wanted me to play in the sand with her and some times she took me down from the wall. She made holes in the sand and covered me up and when I was covered up I jumped out and ran and then came back. Sometimes she let me ride with her Jemima in her Jemima's doll carriage.

CLIMB UP ON A HIGH WALL.

"A woman came out every day to give corn to the hens, and things to the two great cats, and talk to the horses. I did not want the hen's corn. I liked the things that were put into the two great cats' plate, but the dog always wanted what was left. The two great cats had a plate of their own.

"Once when the two great cats were not there and that dog was not, the woman put something in the plate, and went away and I thought I would jump quick and get it, and I raced along the wall and got tangled in a vine, and

jumped, and fell and pulled a great stone down on myself; on the back part of myself; and I could not stir, and when the boy found me and took the stone off, I was a good deal jammed, and I could not walk with the legs which belong to that part. People said I must be killed, but they waited, and I did not have to be killed. I walked with all my legs.

"When I grew bigger I used to go into the Molly girl's house and the woman used to drive me away. She did not like me, for she saw me get into the hen-

house at a place where it was broken, and saw egg-shells I left when I sucked the eggs. I could not eat egg-shells.

"One day I did something bad, though I did not know it was bad. I was in the Molly girl's house. Her Jemima's doll's carriage was on a high place, but the strings hung over. The wind blew hard that day and I was very frisky and I jumped and pulled the doll-carriage down by the strings and broke it, and dragged it about and played with it very long. When the Molly girl came there she cried. The people came and drove me out, and said very loud, '*Scat! scat!*' A cruel boy that heard them *scatting* me set his dog on me, and that dog chased me, but he would not have touched me if the cruel boy had not said, 'Shake her!" When he heard that he took me by the throat. Oh *Dum* and *Dee*, may you never have anything so dreadful happen to you!

"The dog dropped me behind a tree and people found me and said I was dead. The girl I belonged to said I was alive, and they waited, and when they saw the end of my tail stir they put something on the sores the dog made, and the grandma woman took care of me, and I got well. But I would rather have died than to have that cruel boy do so again. Only a cat can know what a cat can suffer from cruel boys. Dogs would not hurt us if people and cruel boys did not tell them to.

I DID SOMETHING BAD.

"One day I had some kittens of my own. We were in a good closet close by my own girl's bed. Oh I was proud of my pretty little dears! I wanted people to come and see them. But when people came they said, ' Why! why! why! The cat has kittens in the closet! Take the cat and kittens away from that closet !'

"They carried us up garret and put us in a box. I would not stay there. I took my kittens one at a time and carried them in my mouth back to the closet. We were put up in the box again and the garret door was kept shut. I got out of the window and carried my kittens down by tree branches, and got in by another window, and soon they found us in the

CARRIED THEM TO THE BARN.

closet. Then the boy put some of my kittens in his hat

and another boy took some and they carried them to the barn, and I went there too; but I would not stay there. I knew what the best place was, the best place was the closet.

"When it was dark I carried my kittens back to the closet. Then they carried us down cellar, and kept the door shut. I found a hole and made it bigger, and squeezed through that hole with my kittens and went back to the closet. They put us down cellar again and stopped up the hole, and kept the door shut.

"One day soon as the door was opened I slipped quick between somebody's feet, and went up stairs to the grandma woman's room, and sat by the fire. The grandma woman looked at me hard and said, 'Poor Pixie! It is too cold for your kittens down cellar; go bring them here.'

"I knew what she said and answered her in my mew language, and went and got my kittens and she made a bed for us in a basket that had room in it.

"When my kittens were big enough to crawl I went away and left them sometimes, and if they cried for my going I punished them. When they were good I let them play with my tail; but I always kept one paw ready to punish them if they bit me, or bit each other. I took great comfort with my dear kittens. They understood everything I said to them. One was taken from me, but I tried to be contented with what were left.

WHERE IT WAS NOT RIGHT FOR KITTENS TO GO.

"They soon grew big enough to follow me all over the house, and I took them to many places. One room was always shut. I did not like that. No cat likes to have a door kept shut.

"One day a woman went in that room and worked and moved the things; and she went away and left the door not shut tight, and I pushed in with my kittens, and they had a happy time. They raced and scampered as if they were crazy kittens, for there was a high wind blowing that day. I tried to keep them out of the bed-curtains, but they would go there. They all got on the bed and raced over the pillows where it was not right for kittens or even cats to go, and they bit the fringes, and jumped up and clawed the tassels and some of the tassels were so good that I clawed them myself. Almost any cat will claw a good tassel hanging down in a windy day. The kittens rolled over each other too near the edge of the bed and rolled off, and hopped up and went scampering round the room pulling all the things they wanted to. They went up on high places and tipped things over, and pulled things down, and got into the drawers, and Pomp heard them, and he came in there and jumped about and pulled things out of the drawers, and gnawed things, and played with my kittens. They would not mind me, and all I could do was to sit in a chair and watch them.

"I thought I heard a mouse in a closet, and went in there to see; and while I was in there somebody drove out my kittens and Pomp. I stayed to see about the mouse, and I ate something bad in that closet. It had been put there for the mice.

"What I ate in that closet made me sick and I was very sick. They gave me medicine. They held my mouth open and put the medicine down my throat with a spoon. I did not like it. I would not take any more. I went away in dark places. Sometimes I crawled into the house, and then they tried to make me eat. They could not make me eat. I gew weaker and weaker, and one day they said I was dead. The boy said, 'That cat is not dead. That is one of the cats that will live all her nine lives.'

"I was not dead, or if I was dead I came to life again.

ONLY TWO.

"When I came to life again two of my kittens were playing by my side. Only two. The others were gone. Very soon even these two were taken from me. Not one of them ever came back. Kittens that have been taken away do not come back.

"Now that I had no kittens to need me at home, I was free to go out and meet my friends on fences and the

THERE I SAW A RAT HANGING BY HIS TAIL.

shed-roofs. I went often, and enjoyed my fights with them very much.

"One day when it was cold weather I went to a swamp

to watch a rat's nest.   Another cat had been watching for
that rat, but I meant to get it myself.   I ran all the way,
and when I got there I saw the rat on the tree holding
on by his tail and eating what he could find, and I went
up, but the rat slipped down the other side and went to
his nest.

"I had better have kept away from that tree.   By going
up that tree I got shot.   Two boys saw me, and one shot
me.   I dropped to the ground.   The boys came and
kicked me.   I was almost dead.   The shots stayed in me
and they are in me now.   I could crawl a little, but I was
very weak.

"While I stayed there, crawling a little when I could,
a cat came out from the swamp and ran at me.   She was
one of my own kittens grown up into a cat.   She had
been dropped in the woods, and she was a wild cat.   She
flew at me and she would have damaged me very much if
a dog had not barked and scared her away.   The dog
did not touch me.   He took me out of a muddy ditch.   I
was crawling, and did not know I was close to the muddy
ditch, and fell into it and went deep in the mud and
water.   The dog jumped in and pulled me out.   He
carried me to a house and dropped me on the doorstep.
The boy came from my house to see me.   The people
said I was dead.   The boy said, 'No, she will come to

HE DROPPED ME ON A DOORSTEP.　　　　　161

life. She is a cat that will live all her nine lives.' And I did come to life. The boy carried me home, and the grandma woman washed me and fed me with milk, and put me in a good bed, and I was soon well enough to take a little squash with my milk.

"The grandma woman used to hold me, and speak softly to me, and if I jumped on her shoulder she never pushed me off and said 'scat!' If I jumped up there when she was eating breakfast she let me stay, and let me taste of her breakfast.

"I wanted to thank the grandma woman, and so one day I brought her a little fish I caught in the pond. I stood on a stone in the pond and looked down close to the water, and when a fish saw my eyes shine sometimes it would jump up, and if I put my paw out quick I could catch the fish. The grandma woman was pleased when I brought the fish, and she wanted to sing to me. I did not like to hear anybody sing. When anybody began to sing I got up and walked all around the room, and scratched at the doors, and I could not keep still. Sometimes the grandma woman sang when I was asleep; but I opened my eyes and began to walk. Sometimes I jumped up and put my paw on her mouth.

"One day the white cat and myself got carried off in a bag. It was going to rain, and we were washing our faces a great deal. A bad boy called us out, and we stopped washing our faces and went out, and he put us in a bag. There were very many cats in the bag. The boy carried us to a place far away and put more cats in the bag, then he carried us to another place and put more cats in, and then he carried us all very far to a strange place and let us all out of the bag in a room and shut the doors and windows tight.

"One of the windows was broken a little and a great cat pushed the glass out, and we all went through, and set off for our own homes in the rain, but I went in a barn and hid till the rain stopped. It took me very long to go home.

"As I passed by a house on my way home, a man in that house was making a noise on a fiddle, and I ran and jumped up on his shoulder, because he was making the noise, and he pushed me off, and I ran, and he threw a wet blacking brush at me, and made a spot on my fur.

"I came home and tried to lick off the spot, but I could not reach it. It is far off and my neck is stiff. Not any cat would lick it off for me. I smelt it all the time and felt it, and it worried me. I could not eat. I grew weak and sick. Sometimes I crawled to the basin and lapped one or two laps of milk, but no more. I did not catch. Mice came near, and I did not even stir the end of my

SHE NEVER PUSHED ME OFF AND SAID, SCAT!

tail. I kept in dark places. I have but little strength left, and with that I am now crawling to the woods to die.

AND LAPPED ONE OR TWO LAPS OF MILK.

Farewell. Beware of guns, beware of dogs, beware of stones, beware of stepping on, beware of shutting up, beware of hot water, beware of drowning, beware of cruel boys, beware of wet blacking brushes. Farewell. You will never see me more.'

"Pixie then crawled to the woods where she was afterwards found dead; so dead that she never came back to life.

"*Dum* and *Dee*, and Mouseroun and Phi, his Wisdom Cat, watched Pixie until she had crawled out of sight. *Dum* and *Dee* then frisked away to catch bugs for the puss with the large family of kittens, and Mouseroun and Phi journeyed on to seek the renowned Mistress Tabby Furpurr, who found out a way of not liking birds, and on that account had her picture taken and set in a pussywillow frame, and who had promised to tell the way to Mouseroun and Phi.

"They did not find her. The renowned Mistress Tabby Furpurr had long lain buried beneath the lilac bush, having died of old age, and alas! without revealing the way she found out of not liking birds!"

"Which was a pity," said the lovely Pussyanita to King Grimalkum as she finished the story, "since now our race must be blamed for liking birds when they cannot help liking them. Blamed, dropped, shot, drowned, stoned — not many of us would be living had we not our nine lives, though not many cats have done to them what was spoken of in the story the cat that hadn't common-sense told at Lady Yellow paw's famous party."

"What story was that?" asked King Grimalkum quickly.

"Nothing your majesty will care to hear," answered Pussyanita. "It is not a common sense story."

"I say I do want to hear it," cried King Grimalkum "I don't want any more common sense stories. I'm tired of common sense. I insist upon knowing what was spoken of in the story the cat that hadn't common sense told at Lady Yellow-paw's famous party."

"Your majesty must understand," said Pussyanita, that probably it never really — "

"I don't care a mouse-ear for your *never reallys*," interrupted King Grimalkum. "I want the story."

"Your majesty's wish shall be obeyed," replied Pussyanita, "but your majesty will perceive at the beginning that it is not a common sense story."

"Make no more words about it!" furiously cried the king, "if you do I'll — "

The lovely Pussyanita made no more words about it, but hastened to begin The Story of the Two Charcoals and the Four Spekkums.

THE STORY OF THE TWO CHARCOALS AND THE FOUR SPEKKUMS.

"There was once a cat who had six kittens of exactly the same size, two very dark ones and four very light ones,

and as she could not think of names for so
many and as it was an important matter,
she spoke to their uncle Thomas about
it. Their un cle Thomas said it was
an impor tant matter, and sent her
to ask the wise and aged Goody Gumbo. Goody Gumbo had seen much and
heard much, for she had been
alive ever since the days
when willow trees bore real
pussys and some said she
was picked off a willow tree
herself.

"Goody Gumbo named the
two dark kittens Charcoal,
and the four light ones Spekkum, and they were after-
wards spoken of as the Charcoals and Spekkums.

"When the Charcoals
and the Spekkums had
grown old enough to run
out-doors, it was seen that
one of the Spekkums
was much too frisky, and

that they all were likely to be.

"Their mother spoke to their uncle Thomas about it and he said, 'send three of them to school to learn to behave and they can teach the other three.

"'Send three of the Spekkums and let Frisky Spekkum be one of the three I will see the schoolma'am.'

"The schoolma'am said that she would teach three of the Spekkums to behave if they would go to the school well dusted in meal bag powder, as she herself always did. Their mother said she would attend to that and three of the Spekkums were sent to school and Frisky Spekkum was one of the three.

"The schoolma'am took them by themselves and talked to

them seriously. She then placed them in a row and said : 'Rule first! Sit straight; tails down; noses up; ears flat; paws hanging!'

"They did so, but Frisky Spekkum did not sit as straight as the others.

"'Rule second! All stand. Ears up; tails up!'

"They did so, but Frisky Spekkum sat down before she was told to. 'If you can't mind,' said the school-ma'am, 'I'll have no more to do with you,' and turned away with a scowl.

"'O, do have something to do with me!' cried Frisky Spekkum, and stood quickly on her feet.

"'I will if you will be good,' said the schoolma'am, and turned back with a smile, and went on with the rules. 'Rule third! Sit straight; ears up; noses down; paws up!'

"They did so, though Frisky Spekkum would not hold her paws as high as the others; and she frisked and caused the others to frisk.

"'When you have learned to make your bows and say good afternoon properly you may go home,' the school-ma'am said. They all made their bows and said good afternoon properly, for all were anxious to go home, and Frisky Spekkum did better than the others, for she was more anxious to go home.

"'Now go,' said the schoolma'am, 'you are a troublesome set and I am glad to be done with you. Scamper home.' And they scampered home.

"On their way home they saw a young rat walking out with his parents, and went behind a wall and peeped through. They wanted the young rat but did not like to touch him when his parents were with him. The young rat was telling his parents of a beautiful shiny box with beautiful cheese in it. His father said 'My child, go not near that beautiful shiny box nor touch that beautiful cheese.'

" The young rat did go to that beautiful shiny box and touch that beautiful cheese and came near losing his life, as my story will soon tell.

"'The three Spekkums went home to dinner, a very good dinner of milk and herring. Their uncle Thomas was there and while they were at dinner a kind girl presented every one of them with a neck ribbon. The Charcoals and the Spekkums went out to play and Frisky Spekkum was naughty and gnawed the others' neck rib-

bons and made them gnaw hers. Their mother spoke to
their uncle Thomas about it and he told Frisky that if
she did not behave he should have to send word to the
rats to carry her away, as they carried away Mab Fizz
Fuzz. She said she was not afraid.

"The two Charcoals went to their uncle Thomas' house
to supper and the four Spekkums stayed with their
mother. When it was supper time their mother said to
them softly, 'Follow me and I will give you something
good.'

"They followed her and she led them to the beautiful
shiny box.

"'You see what is inside,' said she, 'jump quick, when
I lift up the door.'

"The young rat was inside. He had eaten the beautiful cheese and wished to stay no longer in the beautiful
shiny box. He sprang out when the door was lifted. The
four Spekkums sprang after him. They were not quick
enough. He slipped through a rat-hole, though Frisky
Spekkum was near enough to claw his tail as it went
through. He was so frightened he knew not what he
was doing and went straight into a bottle, and there was
something bad left in the bottle, and he would have died
of that if a friendly young frog had not found him. The
young frog's family and the young 't's family had been

NOT QUICK ENOUGH.

175

friends ever since one of the young frog's family saved the life of one of the young rat's family, and that was a long, long time before. It was before the Janjibo.

"But all this belongs to another story and cannot be told now, for there is yet more to tell of the Charcoals and the Spekkums.

"One day their uncle Thomas put on his best clothes and his tall hat and got a sleigh box and two pair of rabbits and invited the Charcoals' and Spekkums' mother to go sleighing with him. Their mother smiled and quickly put on her best clothes and her bonnet with flowers and got her best muff.

"The Charcoals and Spekkums all wanted to go, but their uncle Thomas said so many would be too many for the rabbits and that he would take three and take the other three next time.

"They took three of the Spekkums and told Frisky Spekkum to stay and wait with the two Charcoals and go next time. Their uncle Thomas then helped their mother in, and took his seat, and the three Spekkums hopped in behind and sat looking over the side as happy as they could be. Their mother told them to hold on tight for their uncle Thomas would soon whip up, and they might fall out. Their uncle Thomas whipped up and the rabbits set off upon a gallop.

"Just as they were setting off, Frisky Spekkum ran away from the two Charcoals and climbed up behind the sleigh-box, and held on and tried to get in, but the rabbits went so fast that she fell off and rolled over and over.

"She went back to play with the Charcoals, but she did not behave well. She was too frisky with them. She bit ears, and she almost bit off the two Charcoals' neck-ribbons and made them bite off her neck ribbon and was so frisky that one of the Charcoals would not play, and went away. Frisky then took the other Charcoal with her into pantries and a hen house and other places where cats ought never to go, and made her eat with her thick cream, and custard pie, and other things which cats ought never to eat. They also clawed a best carpet.

"Their uncle Thomas came home and found them in a cheese and butter closet, and they ran, and he ran and caught them by their tails and punished them severely.

"This did not cure Frisky Spekkum. She was still too Frisky. She frisked with tassels, she frisked with whip-lashes, she frisked with reins, she frisked with flies

FRISKY SPEKKUM TRIES TO STEAL A RIDE.

she frisked with rabbits, she frisked with dogs' tails, she frisked with pigs' tails. Her mother told her of Mab Fizz Fuzz who was carried off by her tail by the rats, and told her that if she did not stop being too frisky then rats would have to be sent for. But Frisky would not believe there ever was any Mab Fizz Fuzz, and would not stop

IN A CHEESE AND BUTTER CLOSET.

being too frisky. Her mother spoke to her uncle Thomas about it, and her uncle Thomas said her mother had better send her to Goody Gumbo to be talked to. He said that as Goody Gumbo had been alive ever since real pussys grew on pussy willow trees, she would know how to talk to her.

"Frisky Spekkum was sent **to** Goody Gumbo **to be**

talked to, but when the talking began she made believe
be deaf and not hear a word. Goody Gumbo kept ear-
trumpets for deaf ones and she gave Frisky a heavy
ear-trumpet and made her hold it till the talking was
done.

"After she was talked to by Goody Gumbo, Frisky

GOODY GUMBO TALKING TO FRISKY.

Spekkum was not too frisky for a very long time. She
played with the two Charcoals and the other Spekkums,
and behaved as well as any of them. They were all

quiet and happy, and
Frisky was as quiet
and happy as the oth-
ers. When they were
playing together Fris-
ky made no mischief
with the tails of the
others. She behaved
as well as the others.

"This pleased their
mother very much and
she spoke to their
uncle Thomas about
it. Their uncle
Thomas said he did
not believe that Fris-
ky Spekkum behaved
as well as the two
Charcoals and the oth-
er Spekkums. Their
mother told him to
come and see.

"Their mother
made them sit close
together, in a row,

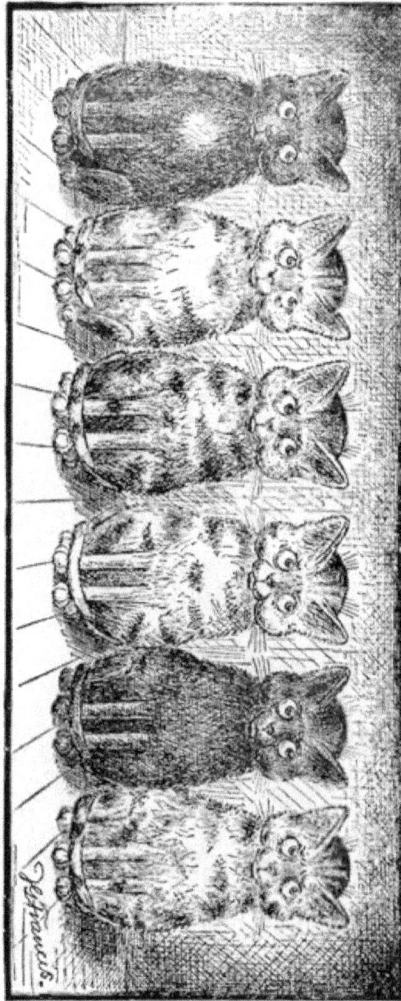

THE CHARCOALS AND THE SPEKKUMS ON THEIR GOOD BEHAVIOR.

with their ears all turned the same way and their eyes all turned the same way, and their tails all turned the same way around their fore paws, and Frisky Spekkum sat so still that when their uncle Thomas came to see he could not tell which one was Frisky.

"Not long after this the same kind girl gave them all new neck-ribbons and their mother said that as they had new neck-ribbons and Frisky had stopped being too frisky, she would have a party. Then she thought it would be a good plan to have them go to singing-school and learn something to sing at the party. She spoke to their uncle Thomas about it and their uncle Thomas said he would try their voices and find out which had voices to sing. He tried their voices and found out that only one of the Charcoals and two of the Spekkums had voices to sing. Frisky Spekkum was not one of the two Spekkums that had voices to sing, and she did not go to the singing school.

"The three that had voices to sing went to singing-

school, and were put in a row by themselves where they
sat very still with their tails around their fore paws as
their mother and their uncle Thomas told them to, and
had their voices tried and were taught to sing the song
of The Two Tailed Mouse, every word of which was as
true as cream.

" The party was to be in a barn-room on account of a
large basket of fish and lobsters which had been placed
there, and it was to be an evening party.

" Before it was time for the party to begin, the three
who were to sing the song of The Two Tailed Mouse,
were told by their mother to go to the barn-room and
sit in a proper manner and sing the song until they could
sing it well enough to sing it at the party and please
all who might hear it. They obeyed her, and as Frisky
Spekkum had not been too frisky for a very long time,
she was allowed to go and hear them sing, if she would
sit still. She sat still a great while, but hearing the singing and looking much at the lobster-feelers made her
want to be too frisky and she frisked with the lobster-
feelers, and went into the basket and frisked with lobster
claws, and gnawed them, and clawed them, and gnawed
and clawed some little fishes, and ate all she could of the
fishes and the lobsters, and made herself sick, and could
not stay up at the party. She had to go to bed in the

hay-
mow,
a n d
when
s h e
w a s
asleep she
dreamed
that her
name was
M a b F i z z -
Fuzz, and that
rats dragged her
off by the tail through a
place that was too small.

"She woke up sorrowful.
She was sorrowful long.
She would not eat, she
would not run, she would
not catch, she would not
play with the two Char-
coals and the other Spek-
kums. Their mother spoke
to their uncle Thomas
about it, and their uncle

FRISKY SPEKKUM'S DREAM.

Thomas said he thought that dream would do Frisky Spekkum good."

"And that is the end of the story, your majesty," said the lovely Pussyanita.

"End?" exclaimed the King. "It has no end. It leaves off short. Why does it leave off short? Why does it not come to a proper end, namely, by the way a cat's tail does?"

"Because, your majesty, it is not a common sense story," replied the lovely Pussyanita. "I told your majesty at the beginning your majesty would not like a story that's not a common sense story."

"I say I do like stories that are not common sense stories!" cried King Grimalkum. "Common sense makes my head ache. Tell me another. Tell the one you skipped; that about the Janjan's."

"Your majesty means The Janjibo," said Pussyanita. "That is the silliest story that ever was."

"I have always wanted to hear the silliest story that ever was," said the King. "Tell it. And let it have an end, or you'll be sorry."

The lovely Pussyanita bowed and began the Story of the Janjibo, and of the Frog and the Rat.

THE STORY OF THE JANJIBO, AND OF THE FROG AND THE RAT.

"Once upon a time, a long time ago, a family of rats made a home for themselves in a haymow, and a good home it was. Corn, and potatoes, and hayseed and other things were handy. With all these good things handy, one of the young rats must needs walk into a trap. Two cats had long been watching the family, and when they saw this young rat go towards the trap, they sprang, and one of them caught him by the end of his tail just as he was going in, and pulled him out, but he got away and ran down-stairs, and the two cats after him, and at the bottom of the stairs he ran into something with a big hole at the big end and a small hole at the small end. He went in at the big hole, and the cats went in at the big hole after him. He went out at the small hole. It was just big enough for him to go through, and was not big enough for the cats to go through, and they turned round quick, and got tangled up in each other, and went out and went

WATCHING THE RAT.

round outside and chased him, but the young rat had

IN AFTER HIM.

jumped out of a window. He was so frightened that he ran, and ran, and ran, across fields and hills, and got lost in a boggy swamp, and a great snapping turtle would have snapped him up, if a young frog had not begged the snapping turtle to let him live. The snapping turtle said he would let him live if the young frog would take care of him. The young frog said he would if his mother would be willing. The young frog's mother said he might take care of him if the young rat would promise not to eat any tadpoles.

"The young rat promised not to eat any tadpoles, and the young frog took care of him and they lived together, and played tag together, and hide-and-seek together, and tiltered together, and did other things together. When the frog hid he croaked for the rat to come and find him, and when the rat hid he squealed for the frog to come and find him. When the frog hid among the cat-o'-nine-tails, the young rat wouldn't play; and when they played tag, if the frog went among the cat-o'-nine-tails the rat wouldn't chase. When they played tilter, they had to tilt high so that the frog's legs need not touch the ground.

"The young rat was happy, and had no wish to return to his family. He went to all the frog concerts, and tried to get the frog tunes, but as he could only squeak them, or squeal them, and could not croak them, he could not get the frog tunes.

"At last his family heard where he was, and begged his aunt to go fetch him home, as she had no children, and could leave home as well as not. His aunt said she

THEY HAD TO TILT HIGH.

193

would go as soon as news should come from the King of
the Cats. The King of the Cats was expected to die. He
had caught a bad cold wading for eels on a damp day, and
had taken to his bed, and
called in Doctor Bowwow, and
Doctor Bowwow had looked
at his tongue and told him he
could not live. The young
rat's family begged his aunt
to go right off. She said she
wished to wait and hear of the
death of the King of the Cats,
for that would be good to
hear.

"As soon as word came
that the King of the Cats was
dead, the young rat's aunt set off to the far-off swamp,
and found it, but by that time the young rat had gone
with the young frog to live on the edge of the pond. She
looked all through the swamp, and got her feet wet, and
lost her way, and tangled herself in the swamp-vines, and
caught herself in a swamp-vine string and could not get
away, and there she stayed until the day of the Wonderful News.

"The Wonderful News was brought by a travelling

kangaroo. As the young rat and the frog were sitting one
evening by the edge of the pond, a kangaroo came leaping past, and stopped between two of his leaps
and said, ' Wonderful News ! Peace between the
cats and the rats and mice ! All friends !' and the
kangaroo leaped on.

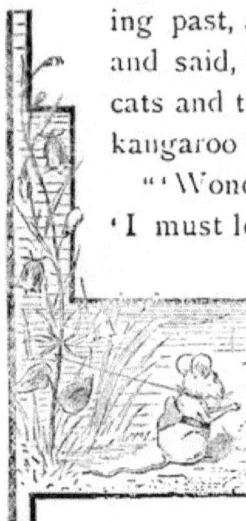

"' Wonderful news indeed !' said the young rat.
'I must let the water rats know.'

"The frog said he would attend to
that, and he got upon a log and croaked,
' Wonderful news ! Peace between
the cats and the rats and mice !'

"Other frogs heard him, and sat
upon logs, stones, rocks and stumps,
and croaked, 'Wonderful news! Peace
between the cats and the rats and mice!' and other frogs
heard these other frogs, and croaked the same, and the
great bull-frogs got hold of it and bellowed it, and frogs
and bull-frogs in other ponds and swamps and bogs heard
it, and croaked it and bellowed it, and before morning the
Wonderful News was known to every water rat far and
near; and the water rats told the land rats as quickly as
they could.

"The young rat's aunt heard it in the swamp, and
jumped hard and broke the swamp-vine string, and set off

on a gallop, this way and that way, and the wrong way, and lost her way, and away she went.

"The young rat said he must travel off somewhere and hear how it all happened, and he and the frog set out together and travelled. Sometimes the young rat let the frog ride on his back, because he could go faster by runs than the frog could by leaps. The rat could not go frog-back, because it was so hard to keep on. When they had travelled a long way they met a mother rat, with her baby in her mouth, running as fast as she could go.

" The young rat asked her to stop and speak to him,

and she stopped. The young rat then asked the mother rat where she was going so fast, and the mother rat said her baby was too sick to be left alone, and that she could not stay away from the Janjibo, and she was carrying the baby to stay at its grandfather's till she should come back from the Janjibo. The young rat asked her what there was to be a Janjibo for.

"She asked him if he had not heard the 'Wonderful News.' He said he had, and that he wished to know how it all happened. The mother rat then said that if they would come to her baby's grandfather's, they could then go with her to the Janjibo, and on the way there she would tell them how it all happened. They went with her to her baby's grandfather's and then to the Janjibo, and this is what the mother rat told.

WHAT THE MOTHER RAT TOLD.

"After the King of the Cats died, and the King of the Cats' son had been made king, the rats and mice sent to ask if the cats and the rats and mice could not be friends, so that there might be peace between them. The new king said he did not think it would be a good plan at all, but he would see what the dogs had to say about it, for dogs had the name of knowing more than cats. He picked out three of his wisest cats, and sent them to the dogs, and the dogs picked out two of their chief dogs, one named Know and the other named Quick, and the two dogs and the three cats met together. Quick asked Know what cats could live upon if they did not eat rats, and mice. Know

THE WISE CATS AND DOGS.

said that if cats should give up catching, then people would feed them more. People kept from feeding them so as to make them catch.

" The wisest of the three wise cats said that dogs were not expected to catch ; they were fed by people.

" Know asked if it was great trouble to catch rats and mice. The next wisest of the three cats said that if he should try it he would find that it was much easier to eat off a plate, or even off the floor, than to sit half

THE PLEDGES OF GOOD FAITH.

the night in a cold barn, or cellar, or garret, tired and hungry, watching rat-holes and mouse-holes. Quick asked if rat-holes and mouse-holes could not be in rooms people lived in where it would be pleasant for a cat to sit and watch. Know said that could not be, for rats and mice did not like people as well as cats did.

"The end of it all was that the dogs thought it would be a good thing for the cats to be friends with the rats and mice, and a little bird that heard all the talk told the Kangaroos.

"In order to be sure that the cats and the rats and mice should do right by each other, the dogs said that the rats must give up a baby rat to be kept by the cats, and the cats must give up a baby cat to be kept by the rats. This was done. The baby rat was youngest of a family of four children, and the baby cat was the youngest of a family of four. The dogs said this would make it even.

"The three cats walked in procession with the baby in front, and their oldest sister walked after them all, and the three rats walked in procession with their baby in front and their oldest sister walked after them all. But when they came in sight of each other, the rats were afraid of the cats and went behind their oldest sister. The oldest sister of the rats then took the baby cat in her mouth, and the cat procession started, and when the oldest sister of the cats came to the baby rat she took that in her mouth and then the rat procession started, and both processions walked away, and the baby rat is now staying with the cats, and the baby cat stays with the rats, and all is well. We do not have to hide in holes and under floors and behind walls, and our children all live to grow up, unless they get sick from eating poison, as my baby did.

"And now that we are all friends, the cats and the rats and mice are going to meet together and have a Janjibo, and there is to be fine music and the tables are to be spread with everything nice. The dogs said that as the rats and mice were the ones to ask to be friends they must be the ones to bring things to eat, and they are working with all their might to get ready the pies, and cakes, and jellies, and ice-creams, and nuts, and sweet corn, and cheeses, and eggs, and dishes, and knives, and forks, and spoons. We shall soon see them. for we are near the place where the Janjibo is to be.

"As the frog and the young rat and the mother rat came near the place where the Janjibo was to be, they saw rats hurry skurrying as fast as they could with cakes, pies, dishes and other things. They met gentlemen rats in their best clothes, carrying knives, forks and spoons, and looking everywhere for eggs.

"Three of these gentlemen rats in their best clothes, found an egg and began to roll it. 'We shall break it doing this way,' said one to the others. 'I am afraid we shall,' said the others, and they stopped to think. The mother rat went to them and said: 'The shells of eggs are too thin. Shells of eggs should be thicker.

"'But I can tell you a way. Let one of you gentlemen lie flat on his back and hold the egg with all four of his legs and let the other two gentlemen draw that one by his tail; then the egg will go safe and the gentleman will get a ride.'

"They did so. The gentleman rat that had the knife gave the knife to the gentleman rat that had the fork and lay down flat on his back, and held the egg in all four of his legs and the other two drew him by his tail and the egg went safe and he got a ride.

"Next came a lively young cat with a pudding-bag string. She said she was frolicking with the rats and was running away with their pudding-bag string. She said she did not care about the Janjibo. She did not care about the peace. She wanted to have a good time. She did not know if she should like to be friends with the rats and mice. Sometimes it was good fun to catch them.

" The mother rat told her that she was very naughty, and the rats could not do without their pudding-bag string and that she must carry it back to them. She did not. She went dancing away with it.

THE CAT RAN AWAY WITH THE PUDDING-BAG STRING.

" Next came a great many rats with a pie so big they could hardly lift it. They were afraid they should drop it, and they held it up with all their might by their heads and their backs, and their shoulders. The Pie-cutter with his knife came close behind. The young rat went to help.

The frog said he should be willing to help, but he should have to go with leaps, and going with leaps was not a good way to go with a pie. The mother rat said to them, 'You'd better set it down and cut it, and then it will be all ready to be passed round. Set it down and cut it, and you can rest while you are cutting it. Cut it first in large pieces, and then cut the large pieces into small pieces. The pie must all be cut in small pieces or there may not be enough to go round.' They set it down, and the mother rat told the Pie-cutter the right way to cut it, and he cut

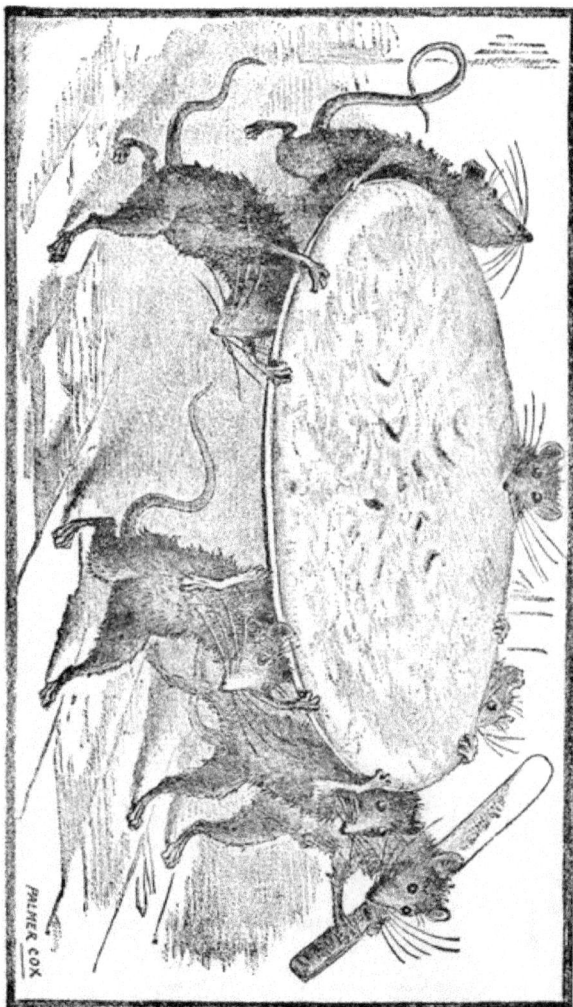

PALMER COX

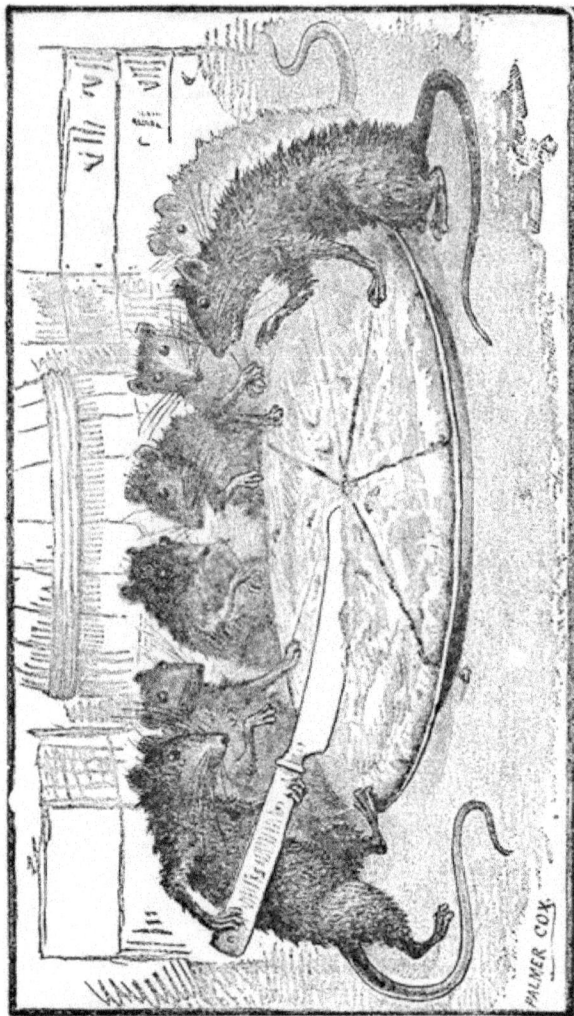

THE MOTHER RAT TOLD THE PIE CUTTER HOW TO CUT IT.

PALMER COX.

it the right way. Just as the Pie-cutter had done cutting it, the young rat looked at a light-colored rat that was among the other ones, and said, 'There's my aunt.'

"It was his aunt. The one that was tangled in the swamp-vine string, and broke it in jumping when she heard the Wonderful News, and got away, and lost her way. She did not find the way she lost, but she found her way to the Janjibo, and was helping.

"'So you are my nephew!' she said. 'How you have grown! Do you know that the cats and the rats and mice are friends?'

"'Oh yes,' said the young rat. 'A travelling kangaroo told me.'

"'Friends indeed!' said his aunt. Look yonder. Do you see what is doing yonder? That is your little brother. Perhaps you never knew that your little brother could take pictures.

"'Never,' said the young rat. 'Can he?'

"'Yes; he can,' said his aunt. 'Yonder he is now, taking the picture of a Tabby. He has plenty to do. There is another close by, waiting for her turn.'

"'Why!' cried the young rat. 'They are the very same ones that chased me when I was a little rat and made me run away!'

"'Yes' his aunt said. 'They are friendly now. What

are you going to do?
Do you want to help
us get ready?'

"'I do,' said the
young rat.

"'Step in here
then,' said his aunt.
'Step in to this Ice-
cream Place, and
stir up the ice-cream.
Stir it up with your
fore paws.' They two stepped into the Ice-cream Place,
and the young rat's aunt showed him how to stir up the
ice-cream with his fore paws. While he was doing this a cat
peeped through the door at him. His aunt thought by the
looks of the cat's eye that it was a cat that had not heard
of the peace.

"She was so afraid the cat did not know of the
peace and would eat the young rat that she caught hold
of his tail quick and pulled him with all her might and
they ran out of the Ice-cream Place by two rat holes.
The mother rat and the frog were waiting for the young
rat and he travelled on with them.

"That cat would not have hurt the young rat. She
did know of the peace and she was gathering up rats for

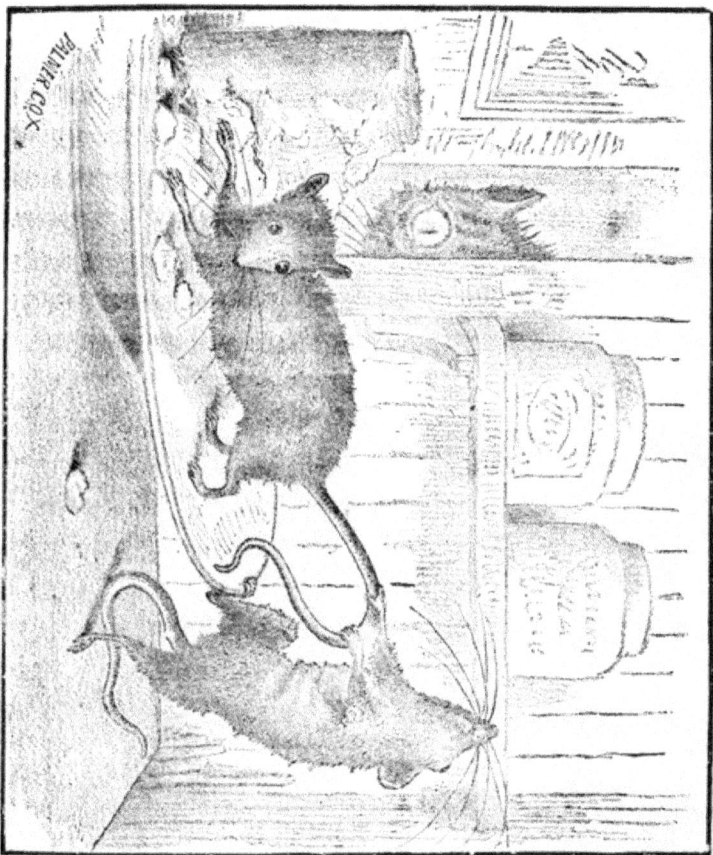

PALMER COX.

AFRAID HE HAD NOT HEARD OF THE PEACE

the Janjibo. The young rat and the frog and the mother rat saw her afterwards showing a great many rats that had come from afar, the way into the Janjibo and even taking up the tired ones in her mouth and carrying them in.

"Three young kittens sat watching her while they waited for their mother. They were dressed in their best clothes

TAKING UP THE TIRED ONES IN HER MOUTH.

and white gloves, all ready to dance a jig at the Janjibo.

"They were waiting for their mother to go in with them. Their mother taught them the jig and she was coming to fiddle for them to dance. They were in a hurry for her to come because they were afraid of a fierce black rat who stood near by with his gun. The fierce black rat had been ordered to stand there with his gnn to keep off the rabbits. The rabbits had been heard to say they did not like the peace between the cats and the rats and mice, and that they meant to break it up, and meant to break up the Janjibo.

"As soon as the mother rat and the frog and the young

rat went into the Janjibo, the mother rat met with her oldest daughter, just from home, and she kept with her mother and the young rat was polite to her.

" A very great number came to the Janjibo. The supper was good, and after supper the ones who could tell stories told stories, and the ones who could sing songs, sang songs, and the ones who could talk, talked.   A mouse

THE SENTINEL

with a lame hind leg said she hoped all cats would know of the peace and told a Spinning Story.

A SPINNING STORY.

· She said that one day when she and her sisters sat spinning in the barn, a cat looked in at the window. They did not run, for why should they run when cats and mice were friends?   The cat that was looking in the window had not heard of the peace and she jumped at them.   Then they ran but she and one of her sisters did not run quick enough, and her sister was bitten in the head and she herself was bitten in the hind leg, and made lame for life.

"Three blind and feeble mice without any tails then told the Blind Mice Story.

THE BLIND MICE STORY.

"They were born blind, and were obliged to find their way by their noses. A farmer's wife had been giving corn to the hens and some of the corn was left in her pocket, and they smelled the corn and ran after the far-mer's wife, and she cut off their tails with a car-ving knife. Now they could not run very fast, for no rat

can run fast unless he feels his tail behind him.

"A cat of the name of Henry, said this story made him think of the Air-Ball Story.

THE AIR-BALL STORY.

"Three kittens, Faw, Sol, and Law, were once playing in a yard when a short boy named Chickerchecker came and tied air-balls to their tails so that he might have the fun of seeing the air-balls take Faw, Sol, and Law up in the air.

"When Faw, Sol, and Law began to feel the back ends of themselves going up they did not know what to do to keep them down and they mewed and mewed and stuck the claws of their fore paws into the ground. Chickerchecker was much pleased.

" Their mother was the other side of the wall and near enough to hear them mew. She knew that if they mewed so, something was the matter. She sprang to the top of the wall and looked over and when she saw what had been done she was very angry, and jumped down, and took the air-balls off of Faw, Sol, and Law's tails and tied them to Chickerchecker, and Checkerchecker went over the wall and blew into a tree.

" Faw, Sol, and Law were so much pleased that they danced up and down. Their mother also was much pleased.

" At the end of this story the singing Tommies sang the funny song of the Bold Young Fishbone and the Gay Young Wishbone.

It began with

> There was a bold young Fishbone,
>> Finnery, finnery fi!
> There was a gay young Wishbone,
>> Winnery, winnery, wi!

and ended in the same manner.

"The singing Tommies had new jackets and trousers and new gloves, as of course any singers would have who were to sing at a Janjibo.

"After this song and others were sung the kittens who came to dance a jig, danced it. Their mother played the fiddle well, and they danced their steps well and gave much pleasure to all present. All present were happy in the peace and no doubt the peace would have lasted to this day if the rabbits and the hens had not broken it up.

"The rabbits and the hens did not like the peace. The rabbits said that cats must eat and if they did not eat rats and mice they must eat rabbits. The hens said that if no rats were eaten they would every one live to grow up and would eat all the corn and the hens and other fowl would wear themselves out scratching for worms. They said they should like to get hold of the frogs, for if the frogs

THEY DANCED THEIR STEPS WELL.

had kept still, so many rats would not have heard the Wonderful News.

"The rabbits said they did not believe the Lion knew of the peace and they meant to send him word and ask him to stop it. The cats would have to do whatever he should say, for the Lion was the head of their family besides being king of all the animals.

"The cat that ran away with the Pudding Bag String was known to think not very well of the peace and she was asked to go and speak to the Lion. She said she would go, but must first borrow her grandmother's boots of swiftness. Her grandmother was just taking her tea and felt very well. She said she was not using her boots and was willing to lend them if they could be taken good care of. The cat that ran away with the Pudding Bag String put them on and went to speak to the Lion.

" The Lion said the peace was the funniest thing he ever heard of, and made him almost die a laughing. He told the cat that ran away with the Pudding Bag String to tell the cats there never could be peace between the cats and the rats and mice, and never should be so long as Lions were Lions, and to tell the rabbits and the hens and other fowl to break up the Janjibo.

" As soon as the rabbits and hens and other fowl heard this they got together from all parts and went leaping and running and flying into the Janjibo, crying 'No peace! No peace! The Lion says no peace.' The hens cackled it, the roosters crowed it, the geese squawked it, the turkeys gobbled it, the guinea fowl squalled it, the peacocks screamed it, and the Janjibo was broken up and the rats and mice ran away quick, for if there was no peace they were in dreadful danger.

THE FROG GOING RATBACK.

·The young rat was in a hurry to get away from the
cats, and the frog was in a hurry to get away from the
hens and other fowl. The young rat said that as he
could go faster by runs than the frog could by leaps, he
would take the frog ratback. The frog threw on a hat
and cloak to hide himself, as he had to sit high, in plain
sight, and got on the young rat's back, and they went so
swift that the frog lost his hat off behind.

"The mother rat and her daughter kept as near them as
they could. When the young rat grew tired he begged
the frog to whip him and make him go fast, for he would
rather be whipped than be caught by the cats.

"He was not caught. They both reached their home
at the edge of the pond, and left that home no more. The
young rat married the mother rat's daughter, and they
had many children, and the frog married the frog he
loved best, and had a large family of little tadpoles, and
the little tadpoles played with the little rats and the little
rats played with the little tadpoles, and the little rats told
rat stories, and the little tadpoles told tadpole stories, and
they all lived happily all their lives."

"And that is the end of the story, your majesty," said
the lovely Pussyanita. "And a good end," said King
Grimalkum. "I knew I should like the story. Is it truly

the silliest story that ever was?" "Yes, your majesty," replied Pussyanita. "The silliest, I mean, of our kind of stories. Of course it is not as silly as the stories the little tadpoles told the little rats."

"Were the stories the little tadpoles told the little rats, sillier than the ones the little rats told the little tadpoles?" asked the king.

"Much sillier," replied Pussyanita.

"Tell them," said the king.

"But your majesty," replied Pussyanita, "there were swarms of little tadpoles and I have not long to live."

"You shall live as long as you can, you lovely creature!" cried the king. "Do you think I would put an end to the life of a sweet young story-teller who can tell both common sense stories and not common sense stories? No! Live! Live and be happy!"

"Alas!" replied the lovely Pussyanita. "I cannot be happy when so many of my kind are in danger. Oh, take back your cruel command! Let our whole race live!"

"I do take it back," answered the king. "For your sake the whole race shall live."

The cruel command was taken back. The whole rac of cats were allowed to live. Those which were "white, or yellow, or which had more white or yellow hairs than dark ones," all these as well as the " black, Maltese and gray," were for Pussyanita's sake allowed to live.

" Here, uncle Fred, is your Cats' Arabian Nights Story Book," said cousin Lucia, "all ready for the children when they shall come next summer with their fathers and mothers; and I hope they will have as much fun in hearing it as I had in writing it."

www.ingramcontent.com/pod-product-compliance
Lightning Source LLC
Chambersburg PA
CBHW030319270326
41926CB00010B/1427